SOCIETY

DAVID FRISBY and DEREK SAYER
Department of Sociology
The University, Glasgow

ELLIS HORWOOD LIMITED
Publishers · Chichester

TAVISTOCK PUBLICATIONS
London and New York

301. 24 FRI

137722

First published in 1986 by
ELLIS HORWOOD LIMITED
Market Cross House, Cooper Street,
Chichester, Sussex, PO19 1EB, England
and
TAVISTOCK PUBLICATIONS LIMITED
11 New Fetter Lane, London EC4 4EE

Published in the USA by
TAVISTOCK PUBLICATIONS
and ELLIS HORWOOD LIMITED
in association with METHUEN INC.
733 Third Avenue, New York, NY 10017

© **1986 D. Frisby and D. Sayer/Ellis Horwood Limited**

British Library Cataloguing in Publication Data
Frisby, David
Society. — (Key ideas in sociology)
1. Social sciences
I. Title   II. Sayer, Derek   III. Series
301   H85

ISBN 0–85312–834–0 (Ellis Horwood Limited — Library Edn.)
ISBN 0–85312–852–9 (Ellis Horwood Limited — Student Edn.)

Phototypeset in Times by Ellis Horwood Limited
Printed in Great Britain by R.J. Acford, Chichester

All Rights Reserved. No part of this book may be reprinted or reproduced or utilized in any form or by any electronic, mechanical or other means, now known or hereafter invented, including photocopying and recording, or in any information storage or retrieval system, without permission in writing from the publishers.

Contents

WITHDRAWN

David **Frisby** is Reader in Sociology at the University of Glasgow, and his most recent publications include *Georg Simmel*, and *The Alienated Mind*. **Derek Sayer** is Lecturer in Sociology at the University of Glasgow. He is the authorof *Marx's Method*, and most recently with Philip Corrigan *The Great Arch*.

Acknowledgements

We wish to thank Pauline Connelly and Pru Larsen for typing the final draft of this monograph.

Editor's Foreword

For a discipline which has such a long history, and which has attracted some of the most original thinkers, it is remarkable that no basic agreement exists in sociology about perhaps its most fundamental concept — the very idea of society itself. This is despite the fact that the term predates the emergence of distinctively sociological thinking in the work of Hobbes and Vico by at least a century. The *Shorter Oxford English Dictionary* gives as 1531 the date of the first usage of the word in its sociological form — 'association with one's fellow men'.

It is commonplace to point out that the concerns of sociology were evident in classical philosophy. Thus, the question of how human society is created and reproduced was not at all foreign to Plato and Aristotle. The rootedness of the question within Western political thought from classical times to the present therefore makes it even more difficult to comprehend why the concept of society has in fact been such a crucial site of intellectual contestation. It is possible, as David Frisby and Derek Sayer point out in their study, to see in all forms of sociological analysis a variety of models of society as either explicit or absent concept. Even those perspectives which deny the existence of a superindividual entity are nonetheless forced to account for actors' understandings of such entities. To treat them as fictional would be to deny the primacy of actors meanings and intentions and undercut the rationale of the methodological individualist perspective.

Thinking about 'society' leads the sociologist directly to what the ethnomethodologists would term 'foundational' questions about sociology. It in part also answers the question of why consensus on the concept of society, and whether it is a necessary or wholly misleading component of sociology, has proved so notoriously difficult to achieve.

David Frisby and Derek Sayer have, in some senses, set themselves an impossible task in this book — for it can be plausibly argued that to provide a conspectus of the variant concepts of society employed in sociology is a task akin to counting the grains of sand on even a very small beach. The success of their book in fact lies in their careful delimitation of the central questions which surround the conceptualization of society. What they do — and do so well — is to set out the ways in which a relatively limited number of ways of thinking about human social structures as collective entities are realistically possible. This method of dealing with the question brings with it another and more fundamental conceptualization — that of the historical specificity of society as a concept itself. To argue that society is distinctively modern, as both social form and concept, is to root thinking about that form quite specifically in the emergence of contemporary capitalist (and thus inevitably also socialist) society.

In arguing that the concept of society is itself intimately tied up with the emergence of a certain distinctively contemporaneous social form, Frisby and Sayer also show how modern professional sociology has by and large been able to get by without an explicit or consensual conception of society. Indeed, the very abstraction implied by the notion of society has put off all but a very few sociologists from attempting to theorize at this level. Only Parsons among recent generations has been prepared to supply the sort of theoretical ideas necessary to thinking at this level. Yet much of his work appears on closer inspection not to theorize society at all, but only the conditions for being social. The concept of social system is not ultimately a definition of society, but a conception of the connectedness of social relations at every level, from the 'micro' to the 'macro'.

This book will represent an indispensable basis for an understanding of the central theoretical dimensions of sociology. In linking the emergence of the concept to the conditions for the appearance of modern society, Frisby and Sayer have made a distinctive contribution to the literature on the key concepts of modern sociology.

Peter Hamilton

Introduction

In the present study we wish to argue for a re-examination of the concept of society in the context of the grounding of sociology as a discipline. To the extent that a theory of society is no longer central to sociology in all its contemporary variants, we have felt it essential to return to the classical grounding of sociology and social theory. But aside from the first chapter which outlines some earlier conceptions of society, our study should not be read as a chronological history of the notion of society.

Rather, what we are interested in is the delineation of key concepts of society that are still significant for modern sociology. How society is conceived or even the terms on which it is not conceptualized crucially affects our conception of how to proceed with sociological analysis and investigation. Where sociology is not grounded in society as an object, we must necessarily raise the issue of what it is that takes its place. In this context, we have chosen not to examine those conceptions of society which instantly reduce it to something else such as a social system. Most notably here, we think of Parsons's assertion that 'society is a special kind of social system'. We have, however, included an examination of those who have not necessarily asked the question 'What is society?' but have nonetheless raised the much more seldom asked one 'How is society possible?' Indeed, it is at least plausible to argue that where the question 'What is society?' has disappeared, the concept of society nonetheless returns, often in a more threatening guise. Those sociologies which have focused upon social interaction and role theory have sometimes been confronted with the unpleasant recognition that the parameters in which they are operating are those of a reified conception of society that is presupposed by their . theoretical starting point. The 'over-socialized concept' of human beings was not confined to those theories which did choose to conceptualize society.

Those who have sought to answer the questions 'What is society?' or 'How is society possible?' have had to confront those issues that remain crucial to the sociological enterprise: how to comprehend facticity and structure, agency, intentionality and meaning, and historicity in the study of social phenomena. Any satisfactory conception of society should be capable of dealing with these problems. Yet the various traditions in sociology have commonly been identified largely with one or the other of these problem complexes or have been judged to have dealt satisfactorily with one or, at most, two of them.

Our study seeks to examine a limited number of instances of attempts to resolve the issue as to the nature of society. It does not pretend to be an exhaustive survey of all the possibilities that sociology has come up with in the past two hundred years. Nor does it attempt to discuss, much less resolve, all the problems associated with the delineation of the concept of society. In fact, it deals with three major complexes. The first is the attempt to ground sociology in an object which is society, making the claim of society's facticity. The second is the grounding of sociology in the study of forms of interaction (Simmel) or social action (Weber) and subsequent developments. Society is largely absent as an object here (though continued by Simmel as a regulative idea), and sociology is seen to deal with individual social actions, interactions and the motives and meanings for action and interaction. In other words, society becomes an assemblage of social actions and interactions in which individual meanings are bestowed upon these actions and interactions. The third problem complex is perhaps the most varied since it deals with society as an idea and an ideal. Society as a collective idea conditioning human activity is to be found already in Durkheim's later writings and, of course, in Peter Winch's conception of society as a set of ideal internal relations. From a very different standpoint, society exists as an ideal counterfactually in all utopian conceptions of society. In this context, we examine recent developments of Critical Theory which argue that we presuppose an ideal community/society in all communication and interaction. Finally, we examine Marx's attempts to develop a critical conception of society which, in a modified form, is capable of both recognizing society as an object and at the same time giving due regard to agency and historicity. Our study concludes with a number of open questions on the development of a theory of society.

1

Society: The Career of a Concept

The fact that in ancient Greece there was no independent word for society should not be taken to imply that, although the ancient Greeks, contrary to popular supposition, did not have a word for it, their philosophers failed to reflect upon society. Over two thousand years later, in fact in 1838, Auguste Comte made public the term 'sociology', which he had already used privately as early as 1824 in connection with his own reflections upon society. Sociology now came to replace that which Comte had earlier termed the *'physique sociale'*. For some time afterwards, sociology came to be not merely the study of society but also the science of society. Yet even by the early part of the present century, sociologists such as Georg Simmel and Max Weber were already seeking to establish their discipline by severing sociology from its identification with society. However much sociology as the study of forms of social interaction or social action might deal with the issue of the process of being a part, or member, of society, it no longer took as its central thematic, as we shall see, the nature of society.

Thus, although the congruence between sociology and the study of society is usually accepted though seldom clearly delineated in answers to the question 'What is sociology?', it is clear that not only is this connection of very recent origin and possibly even superseded, but that reflection upon the nature of society commenced two thousand years before this modern social science constituted itself as an independent discipline.

Such reflections commenced at least as early as Plato's *Republic* in the sense of philosophilizing upon the political society of the *polis,* the city-state and the possibilities for an ideal and just political society that avoided the evils of contemporary political and social forms. But although Plato's *Republic* was highly influential in classical antiquity, it was one of Plato's students in his Academy, Aristotle, who came to produce in his *Ethics* and *Politics* a body of reflections upon the nature of political society, upon human association in general that were to be more decisive for subsequent social and political discourse.

Aristotle's own reflections upon the nature of society converge around the analysis of the forms of human association or community (*koinōnia*) and culminate in the analysis of 'that form of association which is the state' (*koinōnia politikē*) and which takes place in the city state (*polis*) amongst its citizens (*politēs*). The notions of association, community and society are all subsumed under the term *koinōnia*. Hence there exists no separate term for society and the distinctions between community and society and state and society are not in evidence. Indeed, as Runciman has remarked, 'the crucial contrast in Aristotle's mind is not between society and the State but between the private or familial and the political-cum-social' [1]. Nonetheless, in the context of developing a philosophy of that which is political, Aristotle does provide us with a series of distinctions which indicate what is implied by a 'society of citizens', by political society.

Aristotle distinguishes a number of natural associations all of which are 'formed with a view to some good purpose', and the highest of which is 'the association which we call the state, the association which is "political",' namely the *polis* [2]. This association of citizens is to be distinguished from the association of the household (*oikos*) which arises naturally out of the unity of the two 'pairs': 'the union of male and female' and 'the combination of the natural ruler and ruled, for the purpose of preservation' [3], namely, the union of master and slave. The household is then an 'association of persons, established according to nature for the satisfaction of daily needs' [4]. The delineation of the household in this way points not merely to what for Aristotle is a natural hierarchy of husband over wife and master over slave but also to the separation of the economic sphere of the household (and a combination of households) from the political sphere of the *polis*. The association of a number of households constitutes the village, established 'for the satisfaction of something *more* than daily needs'. In turn, the association of several villages is the city state which assures both political and economic independence. Although the *polis* 'came about as a means of securing life itself, it continues in being to secure the *good* life'; it is established by nature as the teleological end of other associations. Hence, 'it follows that the state belongs to the class of objects which exist by nature, and that man is by nature a political animal (*politikon zōon*)'. One important respect in which man is a political animal is through 'the power of speech' and the communication of feelings. More importantly, however, we indicate through language not merely 'what is useful and what is harmful' but also 'what is just and what is unjust. For the real difference between man and other animals is that humans alone have perception of good and evil, just and unjust, etc. It is the sharing of a common view in *these* matters that makes a household and a state.' But this consensus uniting a household and a state should not imply that the two associations are equal since 'the state has priority over the household and over any individual among us. For the whole must be prior to the part' [5].

The emergence of the *polis* does presuppose that the satisfaction of the basic needs and necessities of individuals' lives is already secured. These are satisfied by domestic society and not, as today, by civil society. The *polis* seeks to secure the good life and indeed justice since 'the virtue of justice is a feature of a state; for justice is the arrangement of the political association, and a sense of justice decides what is just'. But central to Aristotle's conception of the political association of citizens in the *polis* is the classification of its inhabitants as free and unfree. Only the free are citizens and they in turn are those who dominate the spheres of labour and economic production of the household. The economic domination over the unfree (slaves), not yet free (children) and the free with less rights (women) is secured by the master, the father and the husband respectively as natural forms of domination. In contrast, the political domination which exists in the *polis* is a domination of the free over the free, requiring not merely the agreement of those so subordinated but also justice secured by law. The *polis* is therefore an association of free and equals based on the principles of law and not upon mere force. What is totally unproblematical for Aristotle is the fact that this just political association of free and equals rests upon the unjust domination of master over slave. Aristotle appears more pragmatic when it comes to the mechanic (*banausos*) or the hired worker (*thēs*) and the admission that 'there must be several kinds of citizen'. However, 'the best state will not make the mechanic a citizen' since 'it is quite impossible, while living the life of mechanic or hireling, to occupy oneself as virtue demands' [6]. Indeed 'a citizen in the fullest sense is one who has a share in honours' associated with holding office in the *polis*. Either the way of life or the insufficient property of the mechanic would probably prevent this taking place.

At all events, what interests Aristotle in his *Politics* is the nature and possibilities of 'political society' within 'society' as a whole. Political society in the *polis* is the association of free and equal persons bound together by a common search for justice secured in law. The forms of justice are examined more fully Aristotle's *Ethics*. One of its significant forms in the light of future conceptions of society is the conception of justice in exchange relations, namely the notion of reciprocal exchange. Here, 'in associations for exchange this sort of justice does hold men together — reciprocity in accordance with a proportion and not on the basis of precisely equal exchange. For it is by proportionate requital that the city holds together . . . it is by exchange that they hold together' [7]. But the community is held together not merely by justice but also by friendship. Only after an elaborate discussion of the forms of friendship does Aristotle begin to examine its relation to society or the community. In a narrower sense, there can exist a variety of communities or societies within the *polis* and in all of them 'there is thought to be some form of justice, and friendship too'. However, 'all forms of community are like parts of the political community' and even though 'religious guilds and social clubs' and the like may be formed for specific ends, they 'all . . seem to fall under the political community; for it aims not at present advantage but at what is advantageous for life as a whole. . . . All communities, then, seem to be part of the political community; and the particular kind of friendship will correspond to the particular kinds of community' [8]. In the political society of the *polis,* the associations of fellow citizens is 'more like mere friendship of association; for they seem to rest on a sort of compact' [9].

This form of practical philosophy of communal or societal existence, based on comparative study and developed by Aristotle, did not immediately generate a continuous tradition of such reflection. Other, universalistic notions of world citizenship were developed by the Stoics and under the Roman Empire the comprehensive union of *nationes* and *gentes* in principle united all human beings as long as they were free and not slaves. However, with the development of Christianity, Aristotle's unity of the community of society of citizens and culture was broken. The *polis* or *civitas* and the church or *ecclesia* were strictly separated, creating, in Augustine's doctrine for example, a dual citizenship of *civitas Dei* and *civitas terrena,* with God and on earth and, accompanying this, obedience to divine and secular laws. Later, this Christian tradition, exemplified in Thomas Aquinas's writings, consolidated a social and political philosophy around the dual problematic of a worldly political society, *communitas civilis,* and that of a divine community that transcended all worldly ones, the *communitas divina.* This problematic served to relativize Aristotle's notion of political life in the *polis* which he had seen as the natural completion of human existence. However, even here and in the early translations of Aristotle's works and concepts, community (*communitas*) and society (*societas*) remained synonymous. Similarly, until the seventeenth century, the notion of society in this broader sense was still associated with friendship as it had been in Aristotle's *Ethics,* with human association as such. Under feudalism there did exist, of course, a division of 'society' into estates, into 'societies' or 'communities' in the narrower sense. The existence and persistence of these estates and of corporations, guilds and the like ensured that the traditional notions of community and society continued to refer to both the political society of the state as well as to units within it. The concept of civil society as distinct from the state emerged only with the disintegration of feudal societies and even then the distinction did not arise unambiguously overnight.

This can be seen in the writings of Thomas Hobbes who, in his early *Elements of Law* (1640), still identifies political and civil society in an unproblematical manner: 'This union so made, is that which men call now-a-days a Body Politic or civil society; and the Greeks call it *polis*, that is to say, a city, which may be defined to be a multitude of men, united as one person by a common power, for their common peace, defence and benefit' [10]. The unity of which he speaks is still that of the natural law kind in the sense that it is naturally real. Only two years later, however, in *De cive* (1642), the notion of this unity has become a fiction. Finally, in his *Leviathan* (1651), it seems that societies do not emerge out of nature. Rather, 'the condition of Man . . . is a condition of Warre of everyone against every one' [11]. Neither the nature of things nor of human beings provides a possible principle for the unification of the natural state of human beings into a civil society. However, it is important to note, along with Macpherson, that this 'natural condition of mankind is within men now, not set apart in some distant time and place' [12]. Hobbes's state of nature in which 'the life of man [is] solitary, poore, nasty, brutish and short' is inferred from existing civilized society and existing desires to live well and 'commodiously'. The causes of the brutish existence of war, in which no man's passions are restrained by a superior power or force, are the dispositions towards competition, diffidence and glory that reside in men. The state of nature therefore refers to the exercise of the unbridled passions and desires of men, unconstrained by law and the enforcement of contracts. Hobbes assumes that 'men are self-moving and self directing appetitive machines' each of whose desire to live well creates a tendency of conflict of each man with every other. Each person's desire is for continuous enjoyment, 'to assure for ever, the way of his future desire. There exists' as 'a generall inclination of all mankind, a perpetuall and restlesse desire of Power after power, that ceaseth onely in Death. And the cause of this, is not alwayes that a man hopes for a more intensive delight, than he has already attained to; or that he cannot be content with a moderate power: but because he cannot assure the power and means to live well, which he hath present, without the acquisition of more' [13]. The acquisition of more is dependent upon appropriating some of the powers of others. This is possible because each man's power is a commodity like everything else: 'The *Value* or WORTH of a man, is as of all other things, his Price; that is to say, so much as would be given for the use of his Power: and therefore is not absolute; but a thing dependent on the need and judgement of another . . . And as in other things, so in men, not the seller, but the buyer determines the Price' [14].

It is a virtue of Macpherson's interpretation of Hobbes's political philosophy to have revealed that this state of nature constitutes a description of a particular form of competitive market society in which every solitary individual is in the market for power, 'every man is opposed to the power of every other man' and those who would be content with a moderate power must rationally strive for more power to protect what enjoyment they have. The market for power, value and honour desired by each participant to its limits necessarily assumes that all will be in conflict with one another. This destructive 'possessive individualism' requires a sovereign power which will regulate such a form of possessive market society. It would be secured because all individuals are equally insecure in an unregulated society and all are, on Hobbes's assumption, in permanently opposed motion to one another. Therefore, all have an equal need for a sovereign power.

Macpherson's reconstruction of Hobbes's possessive market society model not merely brings together in a coherent manner Hobbes's own assumptions about the kind of society he was living in but also serves as a model of society whose foundations were to be called into question in very different ways in succeeding centuries in the works of Locke, the Scottish Economists, the Utilitarians, Marx, Tönnies, Weber, Parsons and many others. This possessive market society postulates that 'there is no authoritative allocation of work', 'no authoritative provision of rewards for work', but that 'there is authoritative definition and enforcement of contracts', 'all individuals seek rationally to maximise their utilities', 'each individual's capacity to labour is his own property and is alienable', 'land and resources are owned by individuals and are alienable', 'some individuals want a higher level of utilities or power than they have' and that 'some individuals have more energy, skill or possessions, than others' [15]. What is noticeably absent from this market model of society is the existence of social classes within civil society as testimony to the fact that 'while every individual in that society is insecure, they are far from equal in insecurity' [16]. The absence of 'the possibility of class cohesion offsetting the fragmenting forces in market society' arises because 'the universality of the competitive struggle between individuals is assumed to have dissolved all class inequalities and all class cohesiveness'. This omission is politically important in that Hobbes is compelled to argue for a self-perpetuating sovereign body or Leviathan rather than look for forms of domination by a property class.

Hobbes's analysis provided powerful argument for a discipline that, unlike natural philosophy whose laws when applied correctly could facilitate 'commodious' living, might discover the laws of human nature 'for a means of the conservation of men in multitudes; and which onely concern the doctrine of Civill Society' [17]. The science of these laws 'is the true and onely Moral philosophy. For Morall Philosophy is nothing else but the Science of what is *Good,* and *Evill,* in the conversation, and Society of mankind' [18]. Its usefulness 'is to be estimated, not so much by the commodities we have by knowing these sciences, as by the calamities we receive from not knowing them' [19]. Hobbes's philosophy is thus firmly and urgently anchored in the tradition of practical philosophy, in which the theory of society is still one element of moral philosophy.

Hobbes was not alone amongst natural law contract theorists in transposing features of existing civil society back into the state of nature in order to demonstrate the natural and rational grounds for establishing a social contract. Drawing back from Hobbes's candour on the nature of human society, John Locke — in *Two Treatises on Government* (1690) and elsewhere — rationally sought to ground civil society in a recognition of the functional importance of the security of life and private property. In Locke's state of nature, men mix their labour (which is itself the property of their own persons) with that which exists in nature. This individual appropriation — for the individual, the fruits of nature 'must be his and so his, *i.e.* a part of him, that another can no longer have any right to it' [20] — must leave enough for others so that they too can exercise their rights to self-preservation and to appropriate nature with their own labour. The same rights hold for not merely the fruits of nature but the earth itself, namely, land. In addition, each individual may appropriate as much of the produce of land and land itself as he can use before it is spoiled. However, Locke, as a good mercantilist, also introduces into this original state that which does not spoil — money — and that which may be treated like land as capital. The produce of land and land itself may both be accumulated as capital, once equal, rational men have decided to place a value on money and thus given their consent to money and unequal possessions. Those without property in the narrow sense of money and land still possess a form of property which is alienable, namely labour. Thus, we have a state of nature which is both a commercial economy and one in which not only is all the land appropriated but wage-labour also exists.

Entry into civil society from the state of nature 'does not create any new rights; it simply transfers to a civil authority the powers men had in the state of nature to protect their natural rights. Nor has the civil society the power to override natural law; the power of civil society and government is limited to the enforcement of natural law principles' [21]. However, Locke carries over from the state of nature assumptions about a society based upon class differentiation which fundamentally affect the natural rights of individuals in civil society. The original mass of equal individuals is transformed into those who possess property and those who in alienating their own persons in wage labour lose full control over their persons and therefore full natural rights. This differentiation is reinforced by Locke's association of accumulation with rationality. Full rationality therefore lies with appropriation rather than with labouring and is something socially acquired in the state of nature.

When these principles are transferred to civil society then we have not merely a justification for a market society but also, with the inherent diffentiation of rationality, the grounds for the creation of a specifically bourgeois public sphere, entry to which is predicated upon the possession of rationality whose index is ownership of property. If the reason for entry into civil society is the preservation of 'Lives, Liberties and Estates' then it is in everyone's interest. But if property is defined as capital then only those with capital are eligible as full members of civil society since 'only they have a full interest in the preservation of property, and only they are capable of that rational life — that voluntary obligation to the law of reason — which is the necessary basis of full participation in civil society' [22]. Thus, whilst all must be brought within the compass of civil society, only a minority could be full members of it in the sense of ruling that society. The latter could 'hand over to civil soceity all their natural rights and powers . . . because the civil society was to be in control of the men of property' [23]. For this group, consent to the formation of civil society was rational. For 'the greatest part of mankind', without leisure for 'learning and logick', without the capacity for rational political action, another future was reserved: to be 'an object of state policy, an object of administration, rather than fully a part of the citizen body' [24].

Over half a century later, Jean-Jacques Rousseau in his *Discourse on the Origin of Inequality* (1758), called into question the method of instituting a social contract for civil society on the basis of extrapolating the need for such a contract from a state of nature. Those 'who have inquired into the foundations of society, have all felt the necessity of going back to a state of nature; but not one of them has got there'. Instead, each such philosopher, 'constantly dwelling on wants, avidity, oppression, desires, and pride, has transferred to the state of nature ideas which were acquired in society; so that, in speaking of the savage, they described the social man' [25], and thus drew us even further away from 'the knowledge of the real foundations of human society'. Instead, Rousseau proceeds through 'conditional and hypothetical reasonings', 'by laying all facts aside' to examine the 'true' state of nature in which 'every man is his own master', in which 'men in a state of nature, having no moral relations or determinate obligations one with another, could not be either good or bad, virtuous or vicious' and in which 'the inequality of mankind is hardly felt, and . . . its influence is next to nothing in a state of nature' [26]. That state is one in which 'man is born free' into a situation in which 'the love of well-being was the sole motive of human action' and men could sustain themselves independently.

Society, for Rousseau, is not something that emerges naturally out of this original state but out of artificial inequalities imposed by social development, and having their origin in social conventions. Foremost amongst these was the conventions surrounding property and inheritance: 'The first man who, having enclosed a piece of ground, bethought himself of saying "This is mine", and found people simple enough to believe him, was the real founder of civil society' [27]. The emergence of inequalities makes human beings dependent upon one another as masters and slaves (in contrast to the development of families in the state of nature in which 'every family became a little society, the more united because liberty and reciprocal attachment were the only bonds of its union'). This dependency upon others 'is without order and stability' [28]. The development of social life through cooperative enterprise, property, agriculture and working metals all produce complex social organizations that involve moral distinctions and substantial inequalities that breed 'every vice'.

Under such circumstances, some way must be found of ensuring that individuals feel that their dependency on the social order is legitimate. This is fulfilled by a social contract grounded in 'the general will' for the common good. Indeed, it is solely on the basis of this common interest that every society should be governed [29]. Such a society is now based upon a 'moral and legitimate' compact in which 'virtue is the conformity of the individual will to the general will'. This aspect of Rousseau's doctrine and much else in it commended itself, amongst sociologists, to Durkheim. The more general advantage of Rousseau's arguments over those of other contract theorists has been expressed by MacIntyre:

> The simple, central, powerful concept in Rousseau is that of a human nature which is overlaid and distorted by existing social and political solutions, but whose authentic wants and needs provide us with a basis for morals and a measure of the corruption of social institutions. His concept of human nature is far more sophisticated than that of other writers who have appealed to an original human nature; for Rousseau does not deny that human nature has a history, that it can be and is often transformed. [30]

Rousseau locates his moral philosophy of the individual firmly within a complex of social relations in society. On occasion he also suggests a sociological answer to the question that was often posed by contract theorists in relation to the body ruling civil society: 'It would be better before examining the act by which a people choose a king, to examine that by which it has become a people; for this act, being necessarily prior to the other, is the true foundation of society' [31].

Was it possible in the eighteenth century to examine 'the true foundation of society' without having recourse to a social contract theory and the assumption that society is merely a collection of individuals whose psychological ends terminate in social institutions? No more succinct dismissal of the whole issue has been provided than in Montesquieu's *Persian Letters* (1721) where he states that 'I have never heard anybody talk of the law of notions but he carefully begun with inquiring into the origin of society; which appears ridiculous to me. If men did not form themselves into societies, if they avoided and fled from each other, it would be right to ask the reason, and to inquire why they kept themselves separate: but they are born united to one another, a son is born near his father, and there he continues; here is society and the cause of it' [32]. However, in his *Spirit of Laws* (1748), Montesquieu not merely establishes his claim to be vitally interested in the nature of human societies but also commences his analysis of forms of law on the grounds that individuals need to be reminded that they live in society. Man, 'hurried away by a thousand impetuous passions . . . is liable every moment to forget himself; philosophy has provided against this by the laws of morality. Formed to live in society, he might forget his fellow-creatures; legislators have, therefore, by political and civil laws, confined him to his duty' [33].

Montesquieu's historical-comparative study of the relationship between types of law and government and types of social organization proceeded on the assumption that however varied practical and historical events and instances might be there exist 'general causes' and a limited number of social types (of forms of government, of laws, etc.). Although a good society for Montesquieu is a just society, the forms of justice do not emerge automatically and human beings must be constrained by custom, law and religion. The forms of association of human beings must be just to be binding. Faced with a multitude of instances of human association in society, Montesquieu sought out the reason for their more limited different types: 'Men are governed by many factors: climate, religion, law, the precepts of government, the examples of the past, customs, manners; and from the combination of such influences there arises a general spirit'. The individual will be shaped by the particular social association in which he or she exists. More generally, political and moral systems are to be judged in terms of the social context in which they exist. For Montesquieu the most important of these were the republican, monarchical and despotic forms of government and society which he examined with considerable sociological insight.

Montesquieu's social analysis greatly commended itself to at least some members of another group of writers concerned with the delineation of civil society — the Scottish moralists. Thus, Dugald Stewart, arguing for the fact that 'man has always been found in a social state', could write that 'so just is the simple and beautiful statement of the fact given by Montesquieu, "that man is born in society, and there he remains" ' [34]. However, such statements mask the full significance of the Scottish enlightenment tradition. The new delineation of civil society by Adam Smith and others as the expanding material sphere of trade and manufacture and, at the same time, as the sphere of activity of private individuals marks a break with the traditional conception of the economy and with the political conception of civil society still adhered to by many natural law and social contract theorists. For Adam Smith and his followers, the economy is no longer limited, as it was in Aristotle, to the household but is an essential element of not merely a 'civil' society but a 'civilized' society that benefits from both 'the disposition to truck, barter and exchange' and the extension of the division of labour and market society. No less significant is the dissolution of any identification of civil society with political society. It is no longer a contract which binds individuals to the state but the interests of individuals and the necessities of society. As David Hume states: 'The general obligation, which binds us to government, is the interest and necessities of society; and this obligation is very strong' [35].

In Adam Smith's case, it should not be forgotten that his *Wealth of Nations* (1776) was, together with *The Theory of Moral Sentiments* (1759), intended to be part of a much wider system of analysis of 'the general principles of law and government, and of the different revolutions they had undergone in the different ages and periods of society' [36]. These broader interests Smith shares with his contemporaries such as Adam Ferguson, David Hume, John Millar and others. Implicit in these interests was an attempt to move away from abstract conceptualizations of natural and social states towards the concrete historical emergence of civil society. This is exemplified, of course, in Ferguson's *An Essay on the History of Civil Society* (1767). Its 'natural history' of man commences from the fact that society is 'a part of the destination of man, joined to the fact, that men are actually found in society'. There exists a wide empirical variety of 'causes' of society though some are given prominence by Ferguson and others. As Ferguson suggests, 'a great work like that of forming society' is 'carried on with a view to the advantages which mankind derives from commerce and mutual support' [37]. Nonetheless, the 'cause' of society cannot be reduced to self-interest. We must examine the development of emotions, rational character and the conflicts which arise between individuals. We cannot return to the origins of society in some natural state 'by supposing a time which never existed . . . since mankind were fairly entered on this scene of human life, there never was any such time; . . both associating and speaking, in however crude a form, are coeval with the species of man' [38]. Indeed illusion of the solitary being so often found in earlier theories may in fact be discovered elsewhere, in the developed civil society. Here, where 'the spirit which reigns in a commercial state' is found is also the place where 'if ever, . . man is sometimes found a detached and solitary being: he has found an object which sets him in competition with his fellow creatures, and he deals with them as he does with his cattle and his soil, for the sake of the profit they bring. The mighty engine which we suppose to have formed society only tends to set its members at variance or to continue their intercourse after the bands of affection are broken' [39]. One decisive force dividing individuals was, for John Millar especially, private property. Its development was intimately connected to the development of civil society and, as he sought to demonstrate in *The Origin and Distinction of Ranks* (1779) — the first 'sociology' of stratification — was a prime cause of the origins of inequality in society. Indeed, property was 'the great source of distinction among individuals'.

Millar did concentrate upon the material forces in society, especially the division of labour which not only contributed to the stratification of civil society but also made workers 'the mere instrument of labour' and reduced them to 'the dupes of their superiors'. Such views on the adverse effects of the detailed division of labour were shared by Smith, who also argued that the worker would cease to use his mental faculties and become 'as stupid and ignorant as it is possible for a human creature to become', and by Ferguson who suggested that 'many mechanical arts . . . succeed best under a total suppression of sentiment and reason', and 'ignorance is the mother of industry as well as of superstition'. This explicit concern for the study of material circumstances and their consequences is well summed up by William Robertson's claim that 'in every inquiry concerning the operations of men when united together in society, the first object of attention should be their mode of subsistence. Accordingly as that varies, their laws and policy must be different' [40]. It also follows from this that not only is civil society to be treated as something distinct from the state but also that the nature of the state might well be conditioned by the forces in civil society. As Ferguson suggests, 'forms of government take their rise, chiefly from the manner in which the members of a state have originally been classed' [41]. This natural history of society thus clearly had a strong sociological component. The history was one which was broadly optimistic despite the deleterious consequences of development. Millar, for instance, was not alone in believing that there exists 'in human society, a natural progress from ignorance to knowledge, and from rule to civilized manners, the several stages of which are usually accompanied with peculiar laws and customs' [42].

This natural progress in society was not necessarily accompanied by clear intentions on the part of actors in society. Some, such as Hume, argued that the principle of 'self-love' of individuals interacting with one another secured general public advantages in society. Smith's notion of 'an invisible hand' in human affairs clearly raises the issue of that which was later to become central to theories of social action in sociology; namely, the significance of the unintended consequences of social action. The pursuit of private interests might promote ends which the individual never intended. In fact, 'nor is it always the worse for the society that it was no part of it. By pursuing his own interest he frequently promotes that of the society more effectually than when he really intends to promote it. I have never known much good done by those who affected to trade for the public good' [43]. The broader issue involved in the unintended consequences of human action is well stated by Ferguson, for whom 'the establishments of men . . . arose from successive improvements that were made, without any sense of their general effect; and they bring human affairs to a state of complication, which the greatest reach of capacity with which human nature was ever adorned, could not have projected; nor even when the whole is carried into execution can it be comprehended in its full extent' [44].

But within the Scottish tradition, it is not merely this aspect of social interaction that is relevant to later developments in social theory. The vision of 'the establishments of men' outlined by Ferguson and their complexity suggests a degree of interdependence between human beings which others also emphasized. Sometimes this was understood in a directly material sense, as when Smith suggests that 'it is not from the benevolence of the butcher, the brewer, or the baker that we expect our dinner, but from their regard to their own interest. We address ourselves, not to their humanity but to their self-love' [45]. More generally, Dugald Stewart, in a manner which anticipates the sociology of Georg Simmel, suggests of the individual that 'before he begins to reflect he finds himself connected with society by a thousand ties, so that, independently of any social instinct, prudence would undoubtedly prevent him from abandoning his fellow creatures' [46]. Smith, in *The Theory of Moral Sentiments,* had already indicated a more sophisticated account of the individual's ties to society that anticipates role theory's discussion of the interaction between self and generalized other. Society is the mirror for the individual's assessment of him- or herself: 'we are anxious about our own beauty and deformity only upon account of its effect upon others. If we had no connection with society, we should be altogether indifferent about either' [47]. More subtly, 'whenever I endeavour to examine my own conduct . . . I divide myself, as it were, into two persons, and . . . I, the examiner and judge, represent a different character from that other I, the person whose conduct is examined into and judged of' [48].

This should suggest that the conception of civil society developed by the Scottish moralists was not merely one that emphasized material circumstances as an important foundation for society but also, to use Smith's terms, the 'moral sentiments' that were necessary in order that a society based upon seemingly self-interested private individuals could continue to function. Exchange and contract require trust and society as a whole cannot exist without justice. Similarly, the complex interaction of classes of individuals and their actions whose products are 'not the execution of any human design' suggests that the negative aspects of this new society, of which Smith, Millar and Ferguson were aware, could become the dominant ones. At all events, the notion of human sociation as the result of the interaction of often contradictory factors which had been developed in the Scottish tradition proved to be important when their works become incorporated into later traditions which viewed civil society itself as a contradictory totality.

If the French Revolution popularized a notion of society as involving the whole of mankind and the destruction of earlier narrower conceptions of civil society, the reaction to the revolution on the part of many romantics led to a resurgence of the concept of community, often as a partnership, and the reduction of society to a notion of sociability. Against this latter restoration philosophy of society must be set Hegel's amplification of the distinction between the state and civil society in which the latter embodied a 'system of needs' and a totality of private individuals. With the gradual emancipation of the Third Estate, civil society came to be conceived as bourgeois society; a society of private individuals composed of free and equal persons and property owners but without the domination of one group by another. A society of private owners divorced from politics and free from the state indicated that instead of political domination, only the economic domination of things (on the basis of the freedom of persons and property) existed in civil society. Such a conception of the separation of the state and civil society broke decisively from the Gaeco-Roman tradition of civil society as political society, a community of citizens (*civitas*) associated with its public-political form (*res publica*), or in other words civil society as bound up with the state.

For Hegel, society consisted by private individuals linked with one another through needs and labour. In the *Jenaer Realphilosophie* (1805/6) and later, this association arises out of language, labour and interaction. The satisfaction of individual needs realized the general needs of society. In other words, the social sphere as the private reproduction of labour and satisfaction of needs of individuals involved a dialectical relationship between private and public spheres. Civil society does become the site of the conflict of social forces but the resolution of such conflicts is still assured for Hegel in their transcendence in the rational universality (and independence) of the state which represents all interests in society. The critique of this relationship between the state and civil society became the task of the Young Hegelians and, of course, Marx.

However, not only were the Young Hegelians reflecting upon the nature of civil society. More ambitiously, Auguste Comte was seeking to establish sociology as a positive science of society that sought out the laws of society in two distinct spheres: social statics as 'the fundamental study of the conditions for existence of society' and social dynamics as 'the study of the laws of its constant motion'. The former required a 'positive theory of order', the latter a 'positive theory of social progress'. That unity of the general and the particular for which not merely Hegel's account of the relations between and within the state and civil society but also his whole philosophical system had striven is abandoned in Comte's positivistic separation. Instead, a 'spontaneous harmony' between the social system and its parts is posited. Yet the aim of the search for the laws of society was not merely to establish sociology as a positive science. Comte sought to counter the tendencies towards social dissolution that had been all too apparent in the French Revolution through a search for the laws of society, including those that might be applied to the integration and subordination of the individual to 'society'. This whole project was itself historically bounded insofar as it was only possible because society and knowledge had evolved to an appropriate state; namely, from the theological, through the metaphysical to the scientific or positive stage of knowledge. To each of these stages of knowledge there correspond particular social orders. In the Three Stages, these prototypes are the family, the state and humankind. Significantly, it is the social whole that is more readily understood than its parts, thereby providing a justification for the study of the evolution of whole societies.

In his social statics, dealing with 'the conditions and laws of harmony of human society', Comte sought to examine 'the conditions of social existence of the individual, the family and society; the last comprehending, in a scientific sense, the whole of the human species, and chiefly, the whole of the white race' [49]. Extended in this way, the earlier conception of civil society dissolves into near universal aggregates. Society is conceived as a social organism within which are social forces that are always 'the product of a cooperation'. These forces are simultaneously material, intellectual and moral. The social dynamics seek to demonstrate the 'natural progress' or evolution of social phenomena: its activity through 'conquest, then defence; lastly industry'; and 'man's social nature' which 'finds satisfaction, first, in the family, then in the state, lastly in the race' [50]. Again, society dissolves into race and serves to illustrate the problem of the total systematization of knowledge through ever more abstract categories.

An alternative systematization was provided by Herbert Spencer whose synthetic philosophy was to unify whole areas of knowledge. The social order and society in particular was seen by Spencer to conform to the natural laws of evolution as the 'change from a state of relatively indefinite, incoherent, homogeneity to a state of relatively definite, coherent, heterogeneity'. This evolutionary tendency present in all phenomena was applied to society itself conceived largely as an organism whose increase in size brings about an increase in its internal differentiation and, at the same time, its integration. Once the parts of the social organism — society — have become more differentiated they become more dependent upon one another. Hence the connection between differentiation, interdependence and integration, one that was challenged by, amongst others, Durkheim. The more complex the society, the more differentiated it is in terms of its parts and the greater the problem of securing a stable interdependence through forms of internal regulation. In the evolution from militant to industrial societies we see the evolution from 'compulsory cooperation' between the elements of the whole society to 'voluntary cooperation', from centralization to decentralization. However, a society could return to its militant state as Spencer seems to have been aware at the end of the century.

The impact of Spencer's evolutionary theory, linked as it was to a growing fascination for Darwinism, cannot be underestimated, least of all in terms of its impact upon sociology and the conception of its subject matter as the study of society as a social organism in which 'the permanent relations among the parts of a society, are analogous to the permanent relations among the parts of a living body' [51]. However, the more universal the scale and scope of the search for the natural laws of evolution of society, the more diffuse, in a sense, the subject matter of sociology became, and the more universalistic became the forces and energies which 'explained' the laws of motion of society. In this context, at the end of the nineteenth century, new attempts were made to ground sociology, though not always in the study of society as an object.

It remains to sketch out a conceptual contrast which had a major impact on both sociological and ideological reflection upon the social world, and which is to be found in perhaps the most systematically misinterpreted classical sociological work, namely Ferdinand Tönnies's *Gemeinschaft und Gesellschaft* (1887). The distinction between community as the embodiment of positive values and society as the site of all that is negative has come to permeate a whole range of social theories, extending from community studies themselves, theories of mass society as well as the neo-romantic conception of communications to be found in the social ideology of Nazi Germany. Somewhat unreflected, it is also to be found earlier in Marx's writings (though not derived from Tönnies), especially with reference to a future communist society. But in terms of the career of the concept of society, what was the nature of Tönnies's distinction between community and society?

In the opening pages of *Gemeinschaft und Gesellschaft,* Tönnies announces that 'society is only a transitional and superficial phenomenon' which must be understood as a 'mechanical aggregate and artefact'. The concepts of community and society are to be applied to 'the historical and contemporary reality of human collective life' in order to express 'the facts of experience'. Society is realized in a number of relationships such as 'indifference', 'hostility' and, above all, contractual exchange relations. Hence, 'the elementary fact of *Gesellschaft* is *the act of exchange* which presents itself in its purest form if it is thought of as performed by individuals who are alien to each other, have nothing in common with each other, and confront each other in an essentially antagonistic and even hostile manner' [52]. The 'decisive factor in the emergence of *Gesellschaft,* that is, *the causative factor* in the tremendous revolution that culminates in *Gesellschaft,* is economic in nature, namely, trade' [53].

Tönnies's conception of society, as he acknowledges, draws upon the earlier work of Hobbes and Marx but focuses upon the arbitrary will formation that the purely contractual relations in society demand. Bourgeois society 'with its most important rule, that everyone can do legally within his realm that which he wishes, but nothing outside' or, in its extended form, as a series of conventions relating to individual freedoms, is thus

> an aggregate by convention and law of nature, . . . a multitude of natural and artificial individuals, the wills and spheres of whom are in many relations with and to one another, and remain nevertheless independent of one another and devoid of mutual familiar relationships. [54]

This may be modified by the formation of 'treaties and peace pacts', even to the point at which 'competition is limited and abolished by coalition'.

In an analogous manner, we can understand 'all conventional society life' whose

> supreme rule is politeness. It consists of an exchange of words and courtesies in which everyone seems to be present for the good of everyone else and everyone seems to consider everyone else as his equal, whereas in reality everyone is thinking of himself and trying to bring to the fore his importance and advantages in competition with the others. [55].

Conventional society is thus understood largely in terms derived from economic society. All the 'creative, formative and contributive activity of man' which is 'akin to art' belongs as it were, to *Gemeinschaft* as a concept.

As many of his contemporaries detected, Tönnies's interest lay not merely in the delineation of the concepts of community and society, but also the cultural tendencies towards communalization and societalization present in modern society. The cultural values and the process of will formation necessary for the development of these tendencies constituted Tönnies's real interest. The ambiguity of his argument in relation to the transitional nature of society (pushed along by the process of rationalization towards socialism and the disintegration of societal tendencies) could enable others to view the nature of society in an even more unfavourable light. Max Scheler, for instance, clearly drawing upon Tönnies's work, maintained that

> 'society' is not the inclusive concept, designating all the 'communities' which are united by blood, tradition, and history. On the contrary, it is only the *remnant*, the *rubbish* left by the inner *decomposition* of communities. Whenever the unity of communal life can no longer prevail, whenever it becomes unable to assimilate the individuals and develop them into its living organs, we get a 'society' — a unity based on mere contractual agreement. When the 'contract' and its validity ceases to exist, the result is the completely unorganized 'mass', unified by nothing more than momentary sensory stimuli and mutual contagion. [56].

Others, such as Max Weber, were to extract more positive results for their own work 'as regards content' from 'the fine work of Ferdinand Tönnies, *Gemeinschaft und Gesellschaft*' [57], by examining the processes of group formation on the basis of communal and societal interests.

REFERENCES

[1] W. G. Runciman, *Social Science and Political Theory*, Cambridge, Cambridge University press, 1965, p. 25.

[2] Aristotle, *The Politics* (trans. T. A. Sinclair, revised by T. J. Saunders), Harmondsworth, Penguin, 1984, p. 54.

[3] Ibid., p. 57.

[4] Ibid., p. 58.

[5] Ibid., p. 60.

[6] Ibid., p. 184.

[7] Aristotle, *The Nicomachean Ethics* (trans. D. Ross, revised by J. L. Ackrill and J. O. Urmson), Oxford and New York, Oxford University Press, 1984, pp. 117–118.

[8] Ibid., p. 208.

[9] Ibid., p. 212.

[10] T. Hobbes, *Elements of Law* (ed. F. Tönnies), Cambridge, Cambridge University press, 1928, p. I, 198.

[11] T. Hobbes, *Leviathan* (ed. and introd. by C. B. Macpherson), Harmondsworth, Penguin, 1958, p. 189.

[12] C. B. Macpherson, *The Political Theory of Possessive Individualism*, Oxford, Oxford University Press, 1962, p. 25.

[13] T. Hobbes, *Leviathan*, op. cit., p. 161.

[14] Ibid., pp. 151–152.

[15] C. B. Macpherson, *The Political Theory of Possessive Individualism*, op. cit., pp. 53–54.

[16] Ibid., p. 85.

[17] T. Hobbes, *Leviathan*, op. cit., p. 214.

[18] Ibid., pp. 215–216.

[19] Cited in C. B. Macpherson, *op. cit.*, p. 103.

[20] Ibid., p. 200.

[21] Ibid., p. 218.

[22] Ibid., p. 248.

[23] Ibid., p. 256.

[24] Ibid., p. 224.

[25] J.-J. Rousseau, *The Social Contract and Discourses* (trans. G. D. H. Cole, revised J. H. Brumfitt and J. C. Hall), London and Melbourne, Dent, 1983, p. 45.

[26] Ibid., p. 64.

[27] Ibid., p. 76.
[28] Ibid., pp. 79–80.
[29] Ibid., p. 182.
[30] A. MacIntyre, *A Short History of Ethics,* London, Routledge, 1967, pp. 183–184.
[31] J. J. Rousseau, *The Social Contract and Discourses,* op. cit., p. 173.
[32] Montesquieu, *Persian Letters* (several editions), 94th Letter.
[33] Montesquieu, *Spirit of Laws.*
[34] L. Schneider (ed.), *The Scottish Moralists on Human Nature and Society,* Chicago and London, University of Chicago Press, 1967, p. 92.
[35] Cited in M. Riedel, 'Gesellschaft' in O. Brunner, W. Conze and R. Koselleck (eds.), *Geschichtliche Grundbergriffe,* vol. 2, Stuttgart, Klett, 1975, p. 838. We have found this the most useful overview of the development of the concept of society.
[36] Cited in 'Introduction' to A. Smith, *The Wealth of Ntions* (Books I–III), (with introd. by A. Skinner), Harmondsworth, Penguin, 1970, p. 13.
[37] L. Schneider (ed.), *The Scottish Moralists on Human Nature and Society,* op. cit., p. 78. In detail, see A. Ferguson, *An Essay on the History of Civil Society,* (ed. and introd. by D. Forbes), Edinburgh, Edinburgh University Press, 1966.
[38] Ibid., p. xxix.
[39] Ibid., p. 80.
[40] Cited in R. Meek, 'The Scottish Contribution to Marxist Sociology', in R. L. Meek, *Economics and Ideology and Other Essays,* London, Chapman & Hall, 1967, p. 37.
[41] Ibid., p. 38.
[42] Ibid., p. 41.
[43] L. Schneider, op. cit., p. 107.
[44] Ibid., pp. xli–xlii.
[45] A. Smith, *The Wealth of Nations,* op. cit., p. 119.
[46] L. Schneider, op. cit., p. 92.
[47] Ibid., p. 71.
[48] Ibid., p. 72.
[49] K. Thompson, *Auguste Comte: The Foundation of Sociology,* London, Nelson, 1976. p. 119.
[50] Ibid., p. 174.
[51] H. Spencer, *First Principles,* London, Williams & Northgate, 1862, p. 176. On sociology see H. Spencer, *The Principles of Sociology,* London, Williams & Northgate, 3 vols., 1885, esp. vol. 1, Part II, pp. 435 ff.

[52] F. Tönnies, 'Zur Einleitung in die Soziologie', *Zeitschrift für Philoso-phie und Philosophische Kritik,* **115,** 1899, p. 242. Our emphasis.

[52] F. Tönnies, *Community and Association* (trans. C. P. Loomis), London, Routledge, 1955. p. 10. Our emphasis.

[54] Ibid., p. 87.

[55] Ibid., p. 89.

[56] M. Scheler, *Ressentiment* (trans. W. W. Holdheim and ed. with introd. by L. A. Coser), New York, Free Press, 1961, p. 166.

[57] M. Weber, *Economy and Society* (ed. by G. Roth and C. Wittich), Berkeley, Los Angeles and London, University of California Press, 1978, pp. 3–4.

2

Society as Object

Along with Karl Marx and Max Weber, Emile Durkheim (1858–1917) is usually seen as one of the three great founders of modern sociology. Unlike them, he had an almost missionary zeal to establish sociology as a distinct science, with an object of its own — society. Durkheim's view of society is not acceptable, or at least not wholly acceptable, to most sociologists today. But the clarity and vigour of his reflections make his work the natural starting-point for any discussion of the modern development of the concept. One many disagree with Durkheim; one cannot ignore him.

Let us begin with an apparent detour: some characteristic remarks of Durkheim's, in an essay of 1914, on what may at first sight appear an odd preoccupation for a sociologist — the immortality of the soul. All human cultures, Durkheim observes, acknowledge a 'constitutional duality of human nature'; 'man has [. . .] everywhere conceived of himself as being formed of two radically heterogeneous beings: the body and the soul' [1]. Although body and soul coexist in the one human being, these are distinct orders of reality, irreducible to one another. Often, indeed, they come into conflict, as any religious believer, fighting the temptations of the flesh, knows. The soul transcends our bodily selves; it is within us, yet not entirely so, a part of us, yet one which partakes also of something infinitely higher. Our bodies are bound to space and time; our souls live on after death.

So 'although the body and the soul are closely associated, they do not belong to the same world':

known to us by sensory experience; the abode of the soul is elsewhere, and the soul tends ceaselessly to return to it. This abode is the world of the sacred. Therefore, the soul is invested with a dignity that has always been denied the body, which is considered essentially profane, and it inspires those feelings that are everywhere reserved for that which is divine. It is made of the same substance as are the sacred beings: it differs from them only in degree. [2]

So universal and permanent a belief as this, Durkheim argues, must testify to something fundamental to the human condition itself. We do indeed lead a 'double existence [. . .] one purely individual and rooted in our organisms, the other social and nothing but an extension of society' [3]. The soul, for Durkheim, is society within us. Its immortality is society transcending us. Sacred beings — the gods — are society personified.

These are commonplaces of Durkheim's sociology of religion. But as interesting, for our purposes, is what Durkheim's sociology of religion reveals about his conception of society itself. For to describe God as society transfigured is also to ascribe to society traditional attributes of divinity.

2.1 SOCIETY AS A REALITY SUI GENERIS

Commenting on his *Rules of Sociological Method* (1895) five years after its publication, Durkheim wrote that 'if we dispense with the detailed rules', this method 'entirely depends on two propositions'. These are '(1) Social facts exist sui generis; they have their own nature. There truly exists a social realm, as distinct from the psychic realm as the latter is from the biological realm and as this last, in its turn, is from the mineral realm'; and '(2) [. . .] for that very reason [this method] must be objective. Social facts must be studied from the outside like other phenomena of nature. *The anthropocentric viewpoint is no better grounded in sociology than in the other natural sciences'* [4].

An insistence on the sui generis character of the social realm is a dominant motif of Durkheim's sociology from start to finish. One of his earliest publications, dating from 1885, asserts that 'Undoubtedly a society is a being, a person' [5]. In 1917, the year of his death, he wrote:

On *society*:
The great difference between animal societies and human societies is that in the former, the individual creature is governed exclusively from *within itself,* by the instincts [. . .] On the other hand human societies present a new phenomenon of a special

nature, which consists in the fact that certain ways of acting are imposed, or at least suggested *from outside* the individual and are added on to his own nature: such is the character of the 'institutions' (in the broad sense of the word) which the existence of language makes possible, and of which language itself is an example. They take on substance as individuals succeed each other without their succession destroying their continuity; their presence is the distinctive characteristic of human societies, and the proper subject of sociology. [6]

Durkheim's claim is that the 'being', society, which is formed out of the association of individuals, is a whole — an object — distinct from and greater than the sum of its parts. It forms a specific order of reality with its own distinctive characteristics. This is what is meant by saying it is sui generis. These characteristics of society are not reducible to nor, therefore, explicable from those of its component elements — human individuals — taken in isolation. Society has emergent properties, that is, properties which do not derive from its elements considered independently of their combination, but which arise from and do not exist outwith that combination itself. The social synthesis, in a characteristically Durkheimian metaphor, is 'chemical' rather than 'mechanical':

The hardness of bronze lies neither in the copper, nor in the tin, nor in the lead which have been used to form it, which are all soft or malleable bodies. The hardness arises from the mixing of them. The liquidity of water, its sustaining and other properties, are not in the two gases of which it is composed, but in the complex substance which they form by coming together. [7]

The relation of society to its component individuals is analogous.

This new, synthetic, higher reality, society, is for Durkheim a part of nature: 'societies are natural entities', and 'social phenomena are natural' [8]. Durkheim consistently opposed what he called 'the dualist prejudice', 'the general tendency to put men and societies outside nature, to make separate disciplines of the sciences of human life' [9]. Here he differs from the interpretive sociologies we will consider in later chapters. At the same time he equally opposed any reductionism that would treat society as an epiphenomenon of human biology or individual psychology. 'For sociology to arise', he writes against what he calls 'materialistic monism',

it was [. . .] not enough to proclaim the unity of reality and knowledge: that unity had also to be affirmed by a philosophy which acknowledges the natural heterogeneity of things. It was not sufficient to establish that social facts are subject to laws. It had also to be made clear that they have their own laws, specific in nature, and comparable to physical or biological laws, without being directly reducible to the latter. [10]

Both the naturalness *and* the distinctiveness of society, in short, are for Durkheim implied in saying it is a reality sui generis.

In fact, for Durkheim, society is the highest being in the natural world. He concludes his last and greatest book, *The Elementary Forms of the Religious Life* (1912), with the ringing declaration that formerly,

> the individual passed as being the *finis naturae* — the ultimate creation of nature; it seemed that there was nothing beyond him, or at least nothing that science could touch. But from the moment when it is recognised that above the individual there is society, and that this is not a nominal being created by reason, but a system of active forces, a new manner of explaining men becomes possible. [11]

For Durkheim recognition of the sui generis reality of society — its distinctive ontological status — is the first, and most indispensable, condition of any scientific sociology. Society is thereby conceived as a 'system of active forces' in its own right, a causally efficacious whole, and sociological explanation is accordingly explanation by specifically social causes.

Durkheim's second essential proposition — that social facts must be studies 'objectively', 'from the outside' — is for him a corollary of the first. He is demarcating himself from two major traditions in social thought here. First, he is distancing himself from aprioristic social philosophy. If, he reasons, the social world is indeed a part (albeit the highest part) of natural reality — a real object, an order of *facts* — then its characteristics and causes can no more be discovered by philosophical speculation than can any other laws of nature. Sociology must be 'positive', not normative; its object is a world 'out-there' which can only be discovered empirically, not deduced from philosophical first principles.

Second, Durkheim is rejecting what he sees as the 'anthropocentric' fallacy: the commonsense notion that since society self-evidently consists of individuals, then the explanation of social phenomena must start and end with these individuals and their motives, reasons, and intentions. For

> if social phenomena are not the work of the isolated individual, if they result from combinations — in which he participates, no

doubt, but into which enter many things other than himself — to know what these syntheses consist of and what their efforts are the scholar must observe, since they take place outside himself. He must face these things in the same state of mind in which the physicist or the chemist faces physicochemical phenomena. That is to say, he must see in them not the expression of individual ideas or sentiments but the product of unknown forces, the nature and mode of whose composition it is precisely a question of determining. [12]

Durkheim describes his method as 'naturalistic', meaning that it adopts 'a mental attitude which is the rule in the natural sciences' [13]. The sociologist 'must embark on the study of social facts by adopting the principle that he is in complete ignorance of what they are, and that the properties characteristic of them are totally unknown to him, as are the causes upon which these latter depend' [14]. The mere fact of being a member of a particular social group, an actor in the social drama, gives no privileged access to the 'laws' which govern it; these are to be discovered by empirical inquiry. If social facts are irreducible to facts about individuals, then it follows that they cannot be known by individual introspection.

Both of these claims — that society is an object, a reality sui generis, and that it must in consequence be studied objectively, 'from the outside' — are encapsulated in Durkheim's famous slogan: 'consider social facts as things' [15]. He is clear that social facts are not material things — for Durkheim, as we will see in more detail in Chapter 4, social life is indeed 'made up entirely of representations' [16]. Rather, 'they are things just as are material things, though in a different way' [17]. What is he saying here? By calling social facts things, Durkheim is drawing attention to two important characteristics which in his view social facts possess.

First, a thing is 'any object of knowledge which is not naturally penetrable by the understanding [. . .] It is all that which the mind cannot understand without going outside itself, proceeding progressively by way of observation and experimentation from those features which are the most external and the most immediately accessible to those which are the least visible and the most profound' [18]. A thing is thus *external* to the mind. Second, 'everything which is real has a definite nature which makes itself felt, with which one must reckon [. . .] [Social facts] are things which have their own existence. The individual encounters them when they are already completely fashioned and he cannot cause them to cease to exist or be different from what they already are' [19]. A thing offers *resistance*; it is not modifiable by mind alone, by a mere act of will.

These characteristics are both encapsulated in the definition of social facts offered in the *Rules*: 'a category of facts which present very special characteristics: they consist of manners of acting, thinking and feeling external to the individual, which are invested with a coercive power by virtue of which they exercise control over him' [20]. Durkheim offers two criteria by which we may recognize social facts:

> *A social fact is any way of acting, whether fixed or not, capable of exerting over the individual an external constraint*;

or:

> *which is general over the whole of a given society whilst having an existence of its own, independent of its individual manifestations.* [21]

For Durkheim the ability to constrain the individual is both an important characteristic of social facts and the principal means by which we may identify them. This ability derives from society's sui generis status, its transcendence *vis-à-vis* individuals. Constraint, here, has a broad compass (for which Durkheim has sometimes — in our view rather trivially — been criticized), but he writes eloquently of what he has in mind. The constraints exerted by legal and moral codes are palpable and manifest in the sanctions that follow if we break them. But the individual is also socially constrained by the facticity of the social world in a multitude of subtler ways:

> If I do not conform to ordinary conventions, if in my mode of dress I pay no heed to what is customary in my country and in my social class, the laughter I provoke, the social distance at which I am kept, produce, although in a more mitigated form, the same results as any real penalty. In other cases, although it may be indirect, constraint is no less effective. I am not forced to speak French with my compatriots, nor to use the legal currency, but it is impossible for me to do otherwise. [22]

Durkheim writes in the same vein of 'social currents' — like, for instance, the 'suicidogenic currents' he analyses in *Suicide* (1897), or the 'collective effervescence' produced by religious or patriotic ceremonial — which 'also possess the same objectivity and ascendency over the individual' and 'come to each one of us from outside and can sweep us along in spite of ourselves' [23]. The manner, form and degree of constraint over the individual, in short, can vary, but the existence of some constraint is an invariant quality of all social facts and a means by which we know them to be social rather than individual.

Durkheim is at pains to point out that this does not imply either that constraint is the sole distinctive property of the social fact, or that coercion is the only or even the most important dimension of the relation of society to the individual. 'For, while institutions bear down upon us, we nevertheless cling to them; they impose obligations upon us, and yet we love them; they place constraints upon us, and yet we find satisfaction in the way they function, and in that very constraint' [24]. Recognition of this dual element in morality — regulation and attachment — is, as we will see, fundamental to Durkheim's substantive theory of society. In modern sociological jargon, society's values and norms are internalized by individuals, to become part of their very personalities. Durkheim stresses the constraining character of the social fact, he says, because social facts may best be empirically *identified* by this characteristic. The qualification is an important one: to use a different vocabulary, it implies a recognition that social rules are as much constitutive as regulative of individual action.

Durkheim's other criterion for identifying the social fact, generality-plus-independence, is rather more complicated. Not all that is general within a society is necessarily social. Something may be general yet appertain to individuals alone, and be explicable by individuals' biological or psychological characteristics rather than any social cause. However, if something *is* social, it will *ipso facto* be general, because it will be externally imposed on all the individuals making up a given group. In this sense Durkheim's second criterion, as he says, simply rephrases the first, for 'if a mode of behaviour existing outside the consciousnesses of individuals becomes general, it can only do so by exerting pressure upon them' [25]. The important point for Durkheim is that phenomena are not social *because* they are general, but the other way around: 'if [a social fact] is general it is because it is collective (that is, more or less obligatory); but it is very far from being collective because it is general' [26].

For certain purposes, Durkheim argues, it may be easier to use this second characteristic to identify social facts than the first, for generality may be palpable where constraint is not. Suicidogenic currents are an example: the constraint Durkheim argues they exert is not empirically manifest in the way it is with, for instance, legal codes, but has to be inferred from the regular association of suicide patterns with other social variables. But the sociologist can (Durkheim contends) readily establish the generality of particular kinds of suicide by using suicide rates, and this generality then provides evidence of the existence of such currents and their capacity to constrain. To do this, however, requires dissociating what is regular and general in the phenomena from what is individual and idiosyncratic, and this is what Durkheim means when he requires that we study social facts independently of their individual manifestations. In the case of suicides, this methodology impels us to look at the statistics of suicide rates rather than the details of individual suicides [27].

In later chapters we will have cause to inquire whether Durkheim has succeeded in identifying what specifically differentiates social phenomena, or as Simmel phrased it, what in society is 'society'. Other sociological traditions have held otherwise. But for the moment, one important footnote to the sui generis theme needs to be recorded. Durkheim frequently draws attention to the fact that society transcends the individual not only in space, but in time as well. Speaking for instance of the categories of reason — space, time, causality, and so on — whose origin he held to be social, Durkheim emphasized that:

> Collective representations are the result of an immense co-operation, which stretches out not only into space but into time as well; to make them, a multitude of minds have associated, united and combined their ideas and sentiments; for them, long generations have accumulated their experience and their knowledge. A special intellectual activity is therefore concentrated in them which is infinitely richer and complexer than that of the individual. [28]

Civilization 'is eminently a social matter, being in fact the product of co-operative effort. It assumes that the generations are linked to each other, and this is possible only in and through society' [29]. Further — and contrary to one common line of criticism, which holds that a Durkheimian perspective is inherently unconcerned with social change — Durkheim fully acknowledges that 'the conditions of social life have changed too much over the course of history for the same institutions always and everywhere to have retained the same importance' [30]. Indeed, he cites such historial variation in defence of the sui generis thesis and against attempts to explain social phenomena by features innate to the human individual and therefore invariant across societies [31].

All this, too, has a methodological corollary, which is not usually mentioned in discussions of Durkheim. In his own words, 'there is no sociology worthy of the name which does not possess a *historical* character' [32]. He expands, replying to a 'Questionnaire concerning sociology' in 1908:

> As for the method appropriate to be used, two words may serve to characterise it: it must be historical and objective.
>
> Historical: the purpose of sociology is to enable us to understand present-day social institutions so that we may have some

perception of what they are destined to become and what we should want them to become. Now in order to understand an institution we must first know its composition. It is a complex entity made up of various parts. These parts must first be known, so that later each one may be explained. But in order to discover them, it is not enough to consider the institution in its perfected and most recent form. Nothing gives us an indication as to the various elements of which it is made up [. . .] It is history which plays this role [. . .] in the order of social realities history plays a role analogous to that of the microscope in the order of physical realities.

It not only distinguishes these elements for us, but is the sole means of enabling us to account for them. This is because to explain them is to demonstrate what causes them and what are the reasons for their existence. But how can they be discovered save by going back to the time when these causes and reasons operated? That time lies behind us. [33]

One may, legitimately, criticize Durkheim's historical practice. It is frequently marred by a simplistic evolutionism. But to focus on society as a historically developing whole, its present states produced by antecedent social causes, seems to us — as it did to Durkheim — to be an inescapable corollary of the sui generis thesis itself. If society is not reducible to the individuals who momentarily inhabit it, its understanding must be historical. And it must remain so even if one accepts the sui generis thesis — as we believe sociologists should — in a form rather different from Durkheim's own.

2.2 SOCIETY AS A MORAL ORDER

We have established that for Durkheim society is a reality sui generis. We need now to ask what kind of a reality he thought it was. One starting point — as for other sociologies also — lies in the Hobbesian problem of order. Given the infinity of conflicting individual desires, objectives, and aspirations, how is social orderliness sustained? Or, as Simmel phrased it, how is society possible? Durkheim's answer, in brief, was that what he called 'social solidarity is a wholly *moral* phenomenon', and society itself specifically 'a moral power' [34]. His views on the subject, however, developed — albeit around a remarkably consistent central core — in ways that are important for his overall conception of society.

In his first major work, *The Division of Labour in Society* (1893) Durkheim distinguishes two kinds of 'social solidarity', *mechanical* and *organic*. Mechanical solidarity is generally characteristic of less advance societies, though it persists in enclaves within modern societies like the military. Its basis lies in the power of what Durkheim called the *conscience collective* — a key concept in his sociology. The French term *conscience* translates both as conscience and as consciousness, and in Durkheim carries both connotations. In *The Division of Labour* he defines the *conscience collective* as 'the totality of beliefs and sentiments common to the average members of a society'. As we might expect, he sees this as 'a determinate system with a life of its own', which 'is independent of the particular conditions in which individuals find themselves' and 'links successive generations to one another'. 'Thus it is something totally different from the consciousnesses of individuals, although it is only realised in individuals' [35]. Because it is supra-individual, a social reality sui generis, the *conscience collective* has the power to coerce that is characteristic of all social facts, and this independence of individuals is the source of its moral authority over them.

Mechanical solidarity rests on a *conscience collective* which, to use Durkheim's own terms, is high in volume, intensity, and determinateness. That is, collective beliefs and sentiments predominate over individual ones, are held with great intensity (and their infraction punished with comparable severity), and regulate people's lives in very detailed ways. The content of these beliefs tends to be both religious and collectivist, elevating society and its interests above those of the individual, while the beliefs themselves are concrete and specific in their stipulations for conduct. Durkheim instances the Pentateuch as an example of such detailed regulation. Mechanical solidarity is a 'solidarity by similarities', based on 'a certain conformity of each individual consciousness to a common type, which is none other than the psychological type of society' [36]. For Durkheim individuation is very much a historical process, not a given: 'if in lower societies so little place is allowed for the individual personality, it is not that it has been constricted or suppressed artificially, it is quite simply because at that moment in history *it did not exist*' [37].

The advance of division of labour destroys the structural (or as Durkheim called them, 'morphological') conditions such solidarity presupposes. Division of labour is itself a process of individualisation, which undermines the possibility of a 'solidarity by similarities', for within it individual life-experiences become more and more differentiated. The *conscience collective* accordingly declines in volume, intensity, and determinateness, its content becomes more secular and more individual-oriented, and its provisions more abstract, general, and imprecise. So what then is the source of social cohesion? Durkheim's answer, at least in 1893, is: in the division of labour itself. Division of labour plays a role equivalent, in modern society, to that once played by the *conscience collective*.

That role, it is essential to realize, remains profoundly a moral one. This is well brought out in Durkheim's critique of Spencer [38]. Spencer also held that it is the division of labour which holds together 'industrial societies', but saw this solidarity as 'no more than the spontaneous agreement between individual interests, of which contracts are the natural expression' [39]. Durkheim argued — devastatingly — that on the contrary, all individual contracts suppose non-contractual and social elements: 'the contract is not sufficient by itself, but is only possible because of the regulation of contracts, which is of social origin' [40]. Such pre-contractual regulation can be seen, for instance, in contract law, but (as Adam Smith had also realized) *any* individual contract rests more fundamentally upon an assumption of trust — or in other words, a shared moral commitment — between its parties. The division of labour is therefore integrative not because it spontaneously harmonizes individual self-interest, but because it constitutes a moral force sui generis which contains that self-interest. Durkheim elaborates:

> We may say that what is moral is everything that is a source of solidarity, everything that forces man to take account of other people, to regulate his actions by something other than the promptings of his own egoism, and the more numerous and strong these ties are, the more solid is the morality. [41]

The division of labour fits this bill. It is a moral force, because through it individuals experience their mutual interdependence, precisely their *social* character. 'This it is that constitutes the moral value of the division of labour. Through it the individual is once more made aware of his dependent state *vis-à-vis* society' [42].

There is thus, for Durkheim, no paradox in the question he asks himself at the outset of *The Division of Labour*: 'How does it come about that the individual, whilst becoming more autonomous, depends ever more closely upon society? How can he become at the same time more of an individual and yet more linked to society?' [43]. Individual specialization and interdependence of individuals — the multiplication of social relations — are two sides of the same coin that is division of labour. Characteristically, Durkheim expresses his thought via biological analogy:

> Society becomes more effective in moving in concert, at the same time as each of its elements has more movements that are peculiarly its own. This solidarity resembles that observed in the higher animals. In fact each organ has its own special characteristics and autonomy, yet the greater the unity of the organism, the

more marked the individualisation of the parts. Using this analogy, we propose to call 'organic' the solidarity that is due to the
division of labour. [44]

After *The Division of Labour in Society,* Durkheim never again
explicitly used the concepts of mechanical and organic solidarity. There is
no space here fully to discuss the subsequent development of his ideas. But
his later writings on the need for 'occupational associations' to regulate the
division of labour imply a qualification of his original view that the division
of labour was a moral force sufficient in itself to ensure solidarity [45].
Certainly he came to think that the *conscience collective* had a bigger part
to play in modern societies than his original sharp distinction between
mechanical and organic solidarity had suggested. The difference between
'segmental' (traditional) and 'organized' (modern) society, in his later
writings, lies less in the strength of the *conscience collective* than in its
content. The wider context for this shift is Durkheim's consuming interest,
after 1895, in religion [46]. He came to see religion as the source and
paradigm of all moral sentiments, and hence — in the specific sense he gave
the term religion — as a feature necessary to all societies, and one
fundamental to all social cohesion, in traditional and modern societies
alike.

In *The Division of Labour* Durkheim had already broached the idea of
'the cult of the individual' as the major remaining integrative value in the
modern *conscience collective.* A residual source of solidarity at that point
in his thinking, this 'cult' was to become a prominent theme of his later
writings. His most poignant development of this argument is to be found in
his article 'Individualism and the intellectuals' (1898), written in the wake
of the Dreyfus affair, which is a passionate defence of individual human
rights against *raison d'état.* Here, significantly, he describes this 'moral
individualism' as a veritable 'religion of humanity'. Once again he attacks
the 'egoism' of Spencer and the Utilitarians, a doctrine he finds 'morally
impoverished':

This ideal so far surpasses the level of utilitarian goals that it seems
to those minds who aspire to it to be completely stamped with
religiosity. This human person, the definition of which is like the
touchstone which distinguishes good from evil, is considered
sacred in the ritual sense of the word. It partakes of the transcendent majesty that churches of all time lend to their gods; it is
conceived of as being invested with that mysterious property
which creates a void about sacred things, which removes them
from vulgar contacts and withdraws them from common circula-

tion. And the respect which is given it comes precisely from this source. Whoever makes an attempt on a man's life, on a man's liberty, on a man's honour, inspires in us a feeling of horror analogous in every way to that which the believer experiences when he sees his idol profaned. Such an ethic is therefore not simply a hygienic discipline or a prudent economy of existence; it is a religion in which man is at once the worshipper and the god. [47]

Moral individualism is not merely distinct from, it is profoundly opposed to utilitarian egoism. For the 'dignity of the individual' does not come from his personal characteristics but from his *common* humanity, from what he shares with others — again, precisely his social character. It implies equal respect for the dignity of others. 'Individualism thus extended is the glorification not of the self but of the individual in general. It springs not from egoism but from sympathy for all that is human.' 'Impersonal and anonymous, such an aim, then, soars far above all individual minds [*consciences particulières*] and can thus serve them as a rallying point. The fact that it is not alien to us (by the simple fact that it is human) does not prevent it from dominating us' [48]. Once again, Durkheim argues that the transcendent character of this sentiment betrays its eminently social origins: 'the religion of the individual was socially instituted, as were all known religions. It is society which fixes for us this ideal as the sole common goal which can rally our wills' [49].

To understand what Durkheim is saying here — and its implications for his overall conception of society — we need to go further into his view of what morality is and how it relates to religion. For Durkheim, all morality has two elements. First, and perhaps most obviously, 'moral rules are invested with a special authority by virtue of which they are obeyed simply because they command' [50]. They are, in other words, obligatory; sanctions attach to them. But second, and for Durkheim equally importantly, morality must be 'not only obligatory but also desirable and desired' [51]. Moral rules specify ideals which individuals aspire to. In carrying out a moral act 'we feel that we dominate and transcend ourselves [. . .] we feel a sui generis pleasure in carrying out our duty simply because it is our duty' [52].

Herein, for Durkheim, lies the link between morality and religion. For, he observes, exactly this duality is also displayed by the idea of *sacredness*: 'The sacred being is in a sense forbidden; it is a being which may not be violated; it is also good, loved and sought after' [53]. 'The sacred object inspires us, if not with fear, at least with respect that keeps us at a distance; at the same time it is an object of love and aspiration that we are drawn towards' [54]. Now division of the world into the sacred and the profane is precisely what, in Durkheim's view, defines religion. Religions are not necessarily or sufficiently characterized by apperception of the supernatural, nor yet by belief in divine beings — there are religions without gods, like Buddhism. Religion is, quite simply, *'a unified system of beliefs and practices relative to sacred things, that is to say, things set apart and forbidden — beliefs and practices which unite into one single moral community called a Church, all those who adhere to them'* [55].

Durkheim offers this clarification of what he means by 'the sacred':

The sacred [. . .] is that which is *set apart*, that which is *separated*. What characterises it cannot, without losing its nature, be mixed with the profane. Any mixture, or even contact, *profanes* it, that is to say, destroys its essential attributes. But this separation does not leave the two orders of being that have been separated upon the same level [. . .] There is between them no common measure, they are heterogeneous and incommensurable; the value of the sacred cannot be compared with that of the profane. [56]

Importantly, sacredness cannot be defined in terms of any features intrinsic to sanctified objects themselves — any object (a cow, a stone, a wooden cross) may be sanctified. What differentiates them as sacred is solely the fact that they have this special *social* status (just as, as Durkheim had earlier argued, the only defining common feature of crimes is that they are socially punished, that they offend the *conscience collective*) [57]. The sacred is, simply, that which is sanctified, transcendent, set apart, whatever this may be.

Morality thus exhibits the same duality as do sacred phenomena, and it is in religion, Durkheim argues, that it has its roots. For him, therefore, 'it is impossible to imagine, on the evidence, that morality should entirely sever its unbroken historic connection with religion without ceasing to be itself [. . .] Morality would no longer be morality if it has no element of religion' [58]. Hence 'religion is, in a sense, indispensable' [59]. Exactly *what* is socially sanctified will vary between societies, but *that* something is sanctified — that religion, in the Durkheimian sense, exists — is fundamental to any social order. The modern order, which makes the human individual as such its sacred object, is no exception: the 'cult of the individual' is merely a secular religion. There is no paradox for Durkheim in this oxymoron. For without morality there is no society, and morality is grounded in the distinction of the sacred and the profane. The key characteristic of moral sentiments is the religious one of the sacred character of the objects to which they relate.

We come now to the crux of Durkheim's argument. What is the source, the hidden content, of the sacred/profane distinction itself? His answer, perhaps, will come as no surprise. The sacred character of moral sentiments, he argues, 'can be expressed [. . .] in secular terms':

> That is, in fact, the distinctive mark of my attitude. Instead of joining with the utilitarians in misunderstanding and denying the religious element in morality, or hypostasising with theology a transcendent Being, I feel it necessary to translate it in rational language without thereby destroying any of its peculiar characteristics. [60]

This 'translation' consists of writing, for God, *society*. The predicates of Divinity, in Durkheim's view, are exactly those — and uniquely those — of society itself. Society is, precisely, transcendent *vis-à-vis* individuals, and by virtue of this transcendence constitutes the sole higher reality capable of inspiring moral sentiments in them. In Durkheim's own, famous words, 'In the world of experience I know of only one being that possesses a richer and more complex moral reality than our own, and that is the collective being [. . .] I see in the Divinity only society transfigured and symbolically expressed' [61]. Religion, then, is society's self-consciousness, and it *accurately* grasps the relation of the individual to society. For

> Society commands us because it is exterior and superior to us; the moral distance between it and us makes it an authority before which our will defers. But as, on the other hand, it is within us and *is* us, we love and desire it, albeit with a sui generis desire since, whatever we do, society can never be ours in more than a part and dominates us infinitely. [62]

From here we may return to Durkheim's reflections on the soul with which we began this chapter. Society's relation to the individual, as Durkheim conceives it, is exactly that of soul to body. Indeed, for Durkheim it is no exaggeration to say that society *is* the human soul:

> While society transcends us it is immanent in us and we feel it as such. While it surpasses us it is within us, since it can only exist by and through us. It is ourselves or, rather, the best part of us, since a man is only a man to the degree that he is civilised. That which makes us real human beings is the amount that we manage to assimilate of this assembly of ideas, beliefs and precepts for conduct that we call civilisation. As Rousseau showed long ago:

deprive man of all that society has given him and he is reduced to his sensations. [63]

Accordingly, 'to love society is to love both something beyond us and something in ourselves. We could not wish to be free of society without wishing to finish our existence as men' [64]. 'The believer bows before his God, because it is from God that he believes he holds his being, particularly his mental being, his soul. We have the same reasons for experiencing this feeling before the collective' [65]. We end on a paradox: that which is most characteristically human in us comes from outside us. Society — this sui generis object, which is irreducible to our individual selves — is the very condition of our individuality.

Durkheim's concept of society has undoubted consistency. The sui generis thesis, as well as being a methodological postulate, underpins the major substantive dimensions of his concept. Society for Durkheim is primarily a moral (and, as we will see in Chapter 4, also a cognitive and symbolic) community because it is an object which is transcendent *vis-à-vis* individuals, both in space and time, and can therefore both coerce them and command their loyalty and respect. For him neither morality nor conceptual thought, both of which go beyond the individual, can originate with the individual; they both testify to and presuppose the ontological distinctiveness of society. Whatever judgement one might finally come to on Durkheim's conception, we should note its immense fecundity. He could not, for instance, have illuminated the social conditions of suicide as he did without first refusing the reduction of the social to the individual: without, in other words, positing society as object. That fecundity, moreover, stems largely from exactly the counter-intuitive aspects of Durkheim's conception, its deliberate distance-taking from the 'common sense' perception of society as nothing but the totality of individuals and their interactions.

That said, there remain evident problems with Durkheim's view. Marxists would argue that he under-emphasizes the material dimensions of society — the rootedness of all social life in humanity's relation with the natural world — and that his stress on moral community neglects considerations both of differential social identity and power and of systemically generated social conflict. They would also contend that in the absence of any concept of contradiction within social structures Durkheim's framework is ultimately unable to deal adequately with social change, despite his own avowed commitment to historical method. Interpretive sociologists would maintain, by contrast, that Durkheim's major fault lies in his failure to grasp intentionality — meaning, motive, purpose — as the distinctive feature of human action, which specifically differentiates the subject-matter of the human sciences and makes methodological 'naturalism' (and any conception of society as object) thoroughly inappropriate. For most interpretivists this entails making the individual far more than the mere residual category it is for Durkheim. Methodological individualists would indeed argue that Durkheim's entire attempt to constitute society as an object sui generis is a misguided and monumental reification, an illegitimate translation of an abstraction into a thing.

We will discuss these views in later chapters, in connection with other conceptions of society. One argument, however, is worth anticipating. The commonest criticism of Durkheim is probably that he 'ignored the individual'. In the words of a classic article, his was 'an oversocialised conception of man'. One might, however, somewhat provocatively argue the contrary: that the problem with Durkheim is less that he had an oversocialized conception of man than an *under*socialized conception of the individual. Throughout his work, Durkheim tended rhetorically to counterpose a sui generis society to an assumed 'pure' biological or psychological individual, and sought to confine sociology to dealing with the former. His own conception of society, however, implies that individuality is itself eminently a social construct. If so, this dichotomy is — in his own terms — simply antediluvian. Social and individual can no longer be opposed like this, because the predicates of individuality are themselves social in character and origin. There simply is no 'pure', pre- or non-social individual which can any longer be counterposed to 'society' in this way.

From here, one might on Durkheim's own premises argue that individual action, precisely because it is a social phenomenon, can no longer coherently be left outside a sociology in the way he attempts. To reconceptualize society — as Durkheim does — as formative of individuals removes the possibility of seeing individual action as a non-social phenomenon. Sociology must therefore deal with meaning and intention at the level of individual action; these too are 'social facts', and therefore not dismissable as mere individualistic residues. This in turn implies that the concept of society itself must then be further developed, in non-Durkheimian ways, to allow individual action to be seen as social, and society, conversely, as existing and working in and through such action. Sociological method, even whilst continuing to recognize the objective facticity of the social realm, might then also look rather different: we would need a hermeneutic, a set of procedures which allowed us to enter into the social construction of meaning. Arguably this line of reasoning is implicit in Durkheim's later conception of society as comprising *représentations collectives*. We will return to this in Chapter 4. But for further insight into the problem of meaning, we must first turn to other sociological traditions, for whom the issue is central.

REFERENCES

[1] 'The dualism of human nature and its social conditions', In R. N. Bellah (ed.), *Emile Durkheim on Morality and Society,* Chicago, Chicago University Press, 1973, p. 150.
[2] Ibid., pp. 150–151.
[3] Ibid., p. 162.
[4] 'Sociology in France in the 19th century', in Bellah, op. cit., pp. 16–17.
[5] Review of Gumplowicz, *Grundrisse der Sociologie.* Quoted in Bellah, op. cit., p. xx.
[6] Extract from *Bulletin de la Société française de philosophie,* **15**, 1917, p. 57, translated in E. Durkheim, *The Rules of Sociological Method,* ed. S. Lukes, London, Macmillan 1982, p. 248.
[7] *Rules,* Preface to 2nd edition, p. 39.
[8] 'Sociology in France in the 19th century'. In Bellah, op. cit., pp. 12, 18.
[9] Ibid., p. 5.
[10] 'Sociology and the social sciences', in *Rules,* pp. 177–178.
[11] E. Durkheim, *The Elementary Forms of the Religious Life,* ed. R. Nisbet, London, Allen & Unwin, 1976, p. 447.
[12] 'Sociology in France in the 19th century', in Bellah, op.cit., pp. 17–18.
[13] Ibid.
[14] 'The method of sociology'. Extract from *Les Documents du progrès,* **2**, Fev. 1908, pp. 131–133, translated in *Rules,* p. 246.
[15] See *Rules,* ch. 2.
[16] 'The method of sociology'. In *Rules,* p. 247.
[17] *Rules,* Preface to 2nd edition, p. 35.
[18] Ibid., p. 36.
[19] Ibid., p. 45.
[20] *Rules,* p. 52.
[21] Ibid., p. 59.
[22] Ibid., p. 51.
[23] Ibid., pp. 52–53.
[24] *Rules,* Preface to 2nd edition, p. 47, n. 4. Cf. his *Sociology and Philosophy,* New York, Free Press, 1974, p. 25, n. 1.
[25] *Rules,* p. 57.
[26] Ibid., p. 56.

[27] See E. Durkheim, *Suicide: a Study in Sociology,* London, Routledge & Kegan Paul, 1970, Introduction and Book II.

[28] *Elementary Forms,* p. 16.

[29] 'The contribution of sociology to psychology and philosophy', in *Rules,* p. 238.

[30] 'Sociology and the social sciences', in *Rules,* p. 185.

[31] See, e.g., *Rules,* p. 247.

[32] 'Debate on explanation in history and sociology'. Extract from *Bulletin de la Société française* de philosophie, 1908, translated in *Rules,* p. 211. Emphasis added.

[33] 'The method of sociology', in *Rules,* pp. 245–246.

[34] 'The determination of moral facts', in *Sociology and Philosophy,* p. 54.

[35] E. Durkheim, *The Division of Labour in Society,* London, Macmillan, 1984, pp. 38–39.

[36] Ibid.

[37] *Division of Labour,* p. 142.

[38] Ibid., Book I, ch. VII.

[39] Ibid., p. 152.

[40] Ibid., p. 162.

[41] Ibid., p. 331.

[42] Ibid., p. 333.

[43] Ibid., Preface to 1st edition, p. xxx.

[44] *Division of Labour,* p. 85.

[45] Ibid., Preface to 2nd edition; *Professional Ethics and Civic Morals* (1904), London, Routledge & Kegan Paul, 1957.

[46] 'It was only in 1895 that I had a clear view of the capital role played by religion in social life. It was in that year that, for the first time, I found a means of tackling sociologically the study of religion. It was a revelation to me. That lecture course of 1895 marks a watershed in my thinking, so much so that all my previous research had to be started all over again so as to be harmonised with these new views'. Letter to the Directeur, *Revue neo-scolastique* (Louvain) **14**, 1907. Translated in *Rules,* p. 259.

[47] 'Individualism and the intellectuals', in Bellah, pp. 44, 45–46.

[48] Ibid., p. 48.

[49] Ibid., pp. 54–55.

[50] 'Determination of moral facts'. *Sociology and Philosophy,* pp. 35–36.

[51] Ibid., p. 45.

[52] Ibid.

[53] Ibid., p. 36.

[54] Ibid., p. 48.

[55] *Elementary Forms,* p. 47.
[56] 'Replies to objections' [to 'Determination of moral facts'], 27 March 1906, in *Sociology and Philosophy,* p. 70. Cf. *Elementary Forms* pp. 36–42.
[57] *Division of Labour,* Book I, ch. II; cf. the discussion of crime in *Rules,* pp. 97ff.
[58] 'Replies to objections'. *Sociology and Philosophy,* p. 69.
[59] 'Individualism and the intellectuals', in Bellah, p. 51.
[60] 'Replies to objections'. *Sociology and Philosophy,* p. 69.
[61] 'Determination of moral facts'. *Sociology and Philosophy,* p. 52.
[62] Ibid., p. 57.
[63] Ibid., p. 55.
[64] Ibid. 'To love one's society is to love this [moral] ideal, and one loves it so that one would rather see society disappear as a material entity than renounce the ideal which it embodies'. Ibid., p. 59.
[65] 'Replies to objections'. *Sociology and Philosophy,* p. 73.

3

Society as Absent Concept

Is it paradoxical that the nineteenth century, which saw the production of programmes for sociology with society as its central problematic as in the work of Comte, Spencer, Durkheim and others, should at its end witness attempts to develop a sociology whose problematic moved increasingly away from society as its object? If sociology were no longer to be understood as the science of society, how was it possible to ground it in such a manner that it could still claim to study this earlier object domain or possibly an even greater one? Such questions are prompted by an examination of those traditions in sociology, originating in Germany in the work of Georg Simmel (1858–1918) and Max Weber (1864–1920) which sought to establish sociology as an independent discipline without grounding it in the ontology of society or a comprehensive theory of society. Instead, they turned to an examination of the process by which individuals engage in sociation (*Vergesellschaftung*) and the forms which they take (Simmel) and the study of collective aggregates such as society as they emerge out of tendencies of social action and the meaningful behaviour of individual actors (Weber). This led them to focus upon the forms of interaction between individuals and groups (Simmel) and the types of meaningful social action which individuals engaged in (Weber). In so doing, this tradition came to emphasize the significance of intentionality, agency and meaning on the part of individuals and groups which arguably are neglected in traditions which took as their starting point either the facticity of society as an independent entity or the evolutionary tendencies in societies contained in comprehensive theories of society.

This tradition of sociology, exemplified in the work of Simmel and

Weber, arose in the context not only of the disillusionment with comprehensive theories of society but also of a radical questioning of the progress dynamics of modern society. In part, this involved challenging current social theories of socialism, many of which still retained a belief in the (often inevitable) progress and dissolution of capitalist society. But equally important in rejecting society as a starting point for sociology was the discovery or even rediscovery of the individual threatened by the unregulated tendencies in modern society. A social theory which ceased to concern itself with the 'laws of motion' of whole societies might well turn to smaller units of investigation — social groups or individuals [1].

Of course, if society as an object is rejected as the ground of sociology then it might be possible to justify sociology within the context of other social sciences in terms of its method. Was it possible to ground sociology in a distinctive method, and especially a method which did not presuppose society as its object? This was attempted by Simmel in the last decade of the nineteenth century.

3.1 SIMMEL ON SOCIOLOGY AND SOCIATION

In the course of the 1890s, Simmel established a foundation for sociology that explicitly turned away from society as an object, as an absolute, hypostatized totality, towards a sociology that was to study the forms of interaction and sociation. In order to demarcate his sociology from what passed for sociology in earlier traditions, Simmel rejects the notion that there exist laws of society and laws of history that are the key to the development of society and history. Indeed, Simmel argues that one cannot speak of laws of social development' since, although there may be discoverable laws for the elements of society, 'for the whole there exists no law' [2]. Similarly, guarding against a conception of sociology as 'the history of society' and against sociology's reduction to a philosophy of history, Simmel asserts that '"laws of history" are not to be found' since like society, history is 'such a hugely complex structure' and 'such an uncertain and subjectively demarcated section extracted from cosmic events, that no unified formula for its development as a totality can be given' [3]. Thus, both the search for the 'laws of motion' of society and history are rejected as aims of sociology.

Not surprisingly, therefore, the notion of society as a general, all-embracing concept is also rejected as the object of sociology. It cannot be the prime object of sociology since 'society is not an entity fully enclosed within itself, an absolute entity, any more than is the human individual. Compared with the *real interaction of the parts* it is only secondary, only the result' [4]. On this view, therefore, society, contrasted with real interactions amongst individuals and groups, is only the name of the sum of these interactions ... It is therefore not a unified, fixed concept but rather a gradual one ... according to the greater number and cohesion of the existing interaction that exist between the given persons. In this manner, the concept of society completely loses its mystical facet that individualistic realism wished to see in it. [5]

Hence, the all-embracing concept of society 'evaporates', leaving behind 'merely a ... constellation of individuals'. In this way,

What palpably exists is indeed only individual human beings and their circumstances and activities: therefore, the task can only be to understand them. Whereas the essence of society, that emerges purely through an ideal synthesis and is never to be grasped, should not form the object of reflection that is directed towards the investigation of reality. [6]

Thus far, Simmel has maintained that society as a comprehensive concept, cannot be the starting point of sociology since it is merely either a term for the sum total of interactions or 'an ideal synthesis'. Instead, sociology should concern itself with the analysis of the real interactions between individuals.

Does this mean that Simmel abandons the concept of society entirely? If we examine Simmel's arguments more closely, then we find that he operates with two conceptions of society, only one of which constitutes the genuine subject matter of sociology. For Simmel, adherence to the broadest conception of society actually hinders the development of sociology. Indeed, 'the internal and external confusion of problems that coalesce in the name of sociology has its root in the notion, that its object is everything which takes place in society' [7]. As such, this already constitutes the subject matter for a multiplicity of social science disciplines. Sociology cannot be defined in terms of 'the contents of social life' but rather upon the 'abstraction of forms of society' upon which these rest 'the whole right of sociology as a distinctive discipline to exist'. These 'forms of society' or, more accurately, forms of sociation and interaction between individuals constitute the real subject matter of sociology.

The problem of grounding sociology as an independent discipline rests, for Simmel, upon an inability to sufficiently distinguish these two conceptions of society. At first sight, it does indeed appear as if society in the broadest sense should be the object of sociology:

> From a great distance, a whole series of personalities and individual acts intermingle and form for the mental eye a concrete mass, Society — just as one from a great distance does not see the single tree of a forest, but sees only the forest .... But, to include such general outlines under the concept of sociology, is to make a faulty distinction between that "society" which is only a collective name arising from our inability to treat singly the separate phenomena, and that society which determines such phenomena through specific forces. We often designate purely parallel phenomena, in a mass, as social, and confuse statistical similarities and synchronisms of a purely individual nature, with those that can be referred back to the real principle of society, the reciprocity of cause. So we do not make the required distinction between that which takes place merely *within* society, as within a frame, and that which comes to pass *through* society. [8]

That which 'comes to pass *through* society' is, of course, the real object of sociology. In other words, sociology 'extracts the purely social element from the totality of human history — i.e. what occurs *in* society — for special attention, or, expressed with somewhat paradoxical brevity, it investigates that which in society is "society"' [9]. Sociology's 'sole object' should therefore be 'the investigation of the forces, forms and developments of sociation, of the cooperation, association and co-existence of individuals'. By the process of abstraction of these 'forces, forms and developments of sociation', sociology gains its distinctive status as 'the only science which really seeks to know only society, *sensu strictissimo*' [10].

This argument rests upon the distinction between two conceptions of society:

> first, the broader sense, in which the term includes the sum of all the individuals concerned in reciprocal relations, together with all the interests which unite these interacting persons; second, a narrower sense, in which the term designates the society or the associating as such, that is the interaction itself which constitutes the bond of association, in abstraction from its material content —

the subject-matter of sociology as the doctrine of society *sensu stricto*. [11]

In this second sense, therefore, society (*Gesellschaft*) is reduced to the process by which we become members of society, the process of sociation (*Vergesellschaftung*).

But before we turn more closely to examine Simmel's grounding of sociology in this narrower sense, we should look again at his broader notion of society. Simmel seeks to guard against the false totalization of society that serves to reify it, and to devalue the significance of its individual elements. For instance, 'the historical method and the theory of evolution in natural science have combined to place the individual within an all-powerful, socio-historical development. The individual appears within it merely as a point of intersection of social fibres ... Thus, society is everything and what the individual adds to its assets is a *quantité negligeable*; he lives from christening presents that his species bestows' [12]. However, just as Simmel is opposed to any conception of natural laws of society as a whole, he also rejects the explanatory power of 'human nature'.

On the other hand, whilst recognizing that individuals and their interactions are what constitute society, Simmel guards against the reduction of the study of social life merely to that of individuals. Thus, he maintains that

I do not believe that one may commence social-philosophical investigations from a more specific definition of society than that society exists there wherever several individuals stand in recipro-cal relationship to one another. For if society is to be an auton-omous object of an independent discipline then it can only be so by virtue of the fact that, out of the sum total of individual elements which constitute it, a new entity emerges; otherwise, all problems of social science would only be those of individual psychology. Yet unity from several elements is nothing other than interaction of the same reciprocally exercised forces of cohesion, attraction, perhaps even a certain repulsion. [13]

However, when Simmel speaks here of society what he has in mind is again this second, narrower sense of society as sociation and interaction that is found 'wherever several individuals enter into reciprocal relations'. Later, and more precisely, Simmel states that 'I see ... society, everywhere, where a number of human beings enter into interaction and form a temporary or permanent unity' [14].

When we come to the larger units of society that we designate as institutions we cannot, because of their complexity, reduce them totally to their individual elements: 'It is thus merely as a methodical aid that we speak of the essence and the development of the state, the law, organisations, fashion, etc., *as if* they were unified essences' [15]. And what of speaking of society itself? In the context of the analysis of exchange relations in a money economy, Simmel still speaks of society in the broadest sense as 'a structure that transcends the individual, but that is not abstract. Historical life thus escapes the alternative of taking place either in individuals or in abstract generalities. Society is the universal which, at the same time, is concretely alive' [16]. Here, society is neither a reified abstraction nor a mere sum of atomistic individuals. Extrapolating from Simmel's earlier arguments, society is 'the totality of ... specific interactions' that does not exist prior to these interactions. Rather, interactions and forms of sociation such as exchange or relations of domination and subordination constitute 'the forms in which "society" comes into being'.

However, Simmel argues that sociology should not commence with the study of society as a totality. Its investigation can only begin once we have researched society in its narrow sense, as forms of sociation and interaction. Only when these forms of sociation and interaction are

investigated in all their manifoldness from their primitive shape to their most complicated development can we gradually solve the riddle, 'What is Society?' For certainly it is not a unified being which lends itself readily to apt definition, but rather consists of the sum of all those modes and forces of association which unite its elements. Society is on the side an entirely abstract general concept which has as little reality as general concepts usually have, the reality from which it is abstracted being the particular socializations; on the other hand it is a summing-up concept (*Summierungsbegriff*) made up of these single threads of association between individuals. [17]

How did Simmel intend to investigate 'these single threads of association', or society in his narrower sense?

Simmel's study of society as sociation rests upon a limited number of axioms. His earliest work commenced from 'a regulative world principle that everything interacts in some way with everything else'. In the social world, this principle directs us to the study of social interaction between individuals and groups. But it is not merely that everything exists in ceaseless interaction; rather also that relationships between things are in permanent flux. Thus, rather than seeing new dimensions of social life as fixed entities we must approach them as processes by means of relational concepts such as interaction, reciprocal effect, sociation and the notion of 'the fundamental interrelatedness of the most diverse phensomena'. The study of social interaction should focus upon the forms of sociation that exist in society by means of a methodical abstraction of the forms of sociation from their particular contents. Society conceived as the ceaseless interaction of its constituent elements provides Simmel with one of his key metaphors for illuminating the complex pattern of interactions: that of society as a labyrinth or web of interactions and relationships. The understanding and explanation of sociation commences from the premise that 'social forces, collective movements' are 'the real and determining' factors in social life and not individual fates. This is true, for Simmel, even though sociology must take account of 'psychological processes' — and he was certainly one of the first sociologists of human emotions — that influence interaction. Thus, the recognition of psychological processes is only a necessary element in sociological research which is directed 'to the objective reality of sociation'.

Sociology thus takes as its subject matter the forms of sociation which 'it treats by means of inductive abstraction .... It is the only science which really seeks to know only society, *sensu strictissimo*' [18]. It intends to be the 'description and determination of the historico-psychological origin of those forms in which interactions take place between human beings' [19]. More ambitiously, Simmel declares that 'if we could exhibit the totality of possible forms of social relationship in their gradations and variations we should have in such exhibit complete knowledge of "society" as such' [20]. Simmel recognizes. however, that sociology is a long way from providing this totality of forms of sociation.

It can also be inferred from Simmel's axioms, and from earlier discussion, that since the social world is characterized by complexity and differentiation, one should approach its investigation without any conception of reducing the totality of forms of sociation to a few simple key types or to a hierarchy of forms. Again, this has a direct bearing upon the relevance of Simmel's study of forms of sociation for the study of society in any broader sense. Sociology, he argues, originally commenced from the apparent 'structures of a higher order':

states and trade unions, priesthoods and forms of family structure, the nature of guilds and factories, class formation and the
industrial division of labour — these and similar major organs and
systems appear to constitute society and so form the realm of
science concerned with it. [21]

However, without denying the existence and significance of such 'major
organizational systems', sociology should be equally, if not more, concerned with less 'structured' constellations of interaction, in fact with
'countless others which, as it were, remain in a fluid, fleeting state but are
no less agents of the connection of individuals to societal existence'. If we
confined ourselves merely to the 'major formations' in society, then 'it
would be entirely impossible to piece together the *real life of society as we
encounter it in our experience*'. Rather, we should examine the 'micro-
scopic-molecular processes' within human sociation since they 'exhibit
society, as it were, *statu nascendi*' [22]. Sociology should investigate the
seemingly insignificant, face-to-face, small-scale interactions and the 'for-
tuitous fragments' of sociation:

On every day, at every hour, such threads are spun, are allowed to
fall, are taken up again, replaced by others intertwined with
others. Here lie the interactions ... between the atoms of society
which bear the whole tenacity and elasticity, the whole colourful-
ness and unity of this so evident and so puzzling life of society. [23]

Hence, in order to obtain a 'deeper and more accurate' understanding of
society,

we can no longer take to be unimportant consideration of the
delicate, invisible threads that are woven between one person and
another if we wish to grasp the web of society according to its
productive, form-giving forces; hitherto, sociology has largely
been concerned to describe this web only with regard to the finally
created pattern of its highest manifest levels. [24]

These 'delicate, invisible threads' are only accessible through a 'psychological microscopy' that is sensitive to the slightest nuance of social interaction.

How far Simmel's sociology concerns itself with society as sociation, as interaction, may be guaged, for example, not merely from his analysis of exchange as a pure form of sociation — indeed as 'a sociological phenomenon *sui generis*' — but also from '*the play form of sociation*': sociability (*Geselligkeit*); like other forms of sociation, it does not derive its existence from society. For instance, 'superiority and inferiority is by no means a formation necessarily subsequent to the existence of "society". It is rather one of the forms in which "society" comes into being' [25]. But more than this, sociability constitutes *the* pure form of sociation. Sociability itself 'plays at the forms of society'. It is not something *made* by society, it *is* society in a pure sense:

> The political, the economic, the purposive society of any sort is, to be sure, always 'society'. But only the sociable gathering is 'a society' without further qualification, because it alone represents the pure abstract play of from, all the specific contents of the one-sided and qualified 'societies' being dissolved away. [26]

Indeed, 'everything may be subsumed under sociability which one can call sociological play-form', the 'social game'. For Simmel, however, 'the social game has a deeper double meaning — that it is played not only *in* a society as its outward bearer but that with its help people actually 'play' 'society' [27]. And clearly what interests Simmel is society as sociation, not least because 'the interaction between individuals is the starting point of all social formations' [28]. Sociology's task is to investigate the various forms that sociation takes, whether it be sociability or conflict, domination and subordination, and so on.

In fact, Simmel's major sociological work, his *Soziologie* (1908), is subtitled 'Investigations of the Forms of Sociation'. And just as over a decade earlier he had argued that an answer to the question 'What is society?' could not be given until the multiplicity and diversity of forms of sociation had been studied sociologically, so too does his *Soziologie* disclaim any systematic and definitive answer to this question. However, what is new is an outline of an answer to a different question, namely, 'How is society possible?' In this context, the whole of Simmel's study of forms of sociation is 'in a certain sense, ... the beginning of the answer to this question. For it inquires into the processes .... that condition the existence of individuals as society' [29]. Simmel's study of the forms of sociation does not view them as the 'antecedent causes' of society but as 'part of the synthesis to which we give the inclusive name of "society". And lest

Simmel's question 'How is society possible?' be misconstrued in purely Kantian terms, Simmel insists that 'the unity of society needs no observer. It is directly realized by its own elements because those elements are themselves conscious and synthesizing units'. Simmel thus seeks to guard against treating society either as a 'real product' or as a 'purely transcendental presupposition of sociological experience'.

The 'existence of individuals as society' obviously presupposes that individuals do not merely exist as empirical atoms or mere egos. With an echo of the late Durkheim and anticipating Mead and others, Simmel identifies society as 'my representation' of myself and others, not merely as 'I' but also as 'you', in such a way that 'we feel the *you* as something independent of our representation of it, as something that exists with exactly the same autonomy as does our own existence. And yet, this selfness of the other does not preclude his being made our representation' [30]. However, it should by now be clear once more that Simmel is identifying society with sociation. The answer to the question 'How is society possible?', is 'an inquiry into the conditions of the process of sociation' [31].

There exists a further important aspect of Simmel's inquiry, namely that the three aprioris of sociation — which Gerhardt has termed those of 'role', 'individuality' and 'structure' — constitute part of 'the *epistemology* of society' [32]. It is an inquiry into 'the consciousness of sociating or of being sociated' which is 'the immediate agent, the inner significance, of sociation itself. It is the processes of interaction which signify the fact of being sociated to the individual'. Within the context of these presuppositions, Simmel outlines his three aprioris of sociation. The *first* apriori is the social mediation of action insofar as action is always social action. The relation between actors is the product of social abstraction since our knowledge of the other person and their individuality is always incomplete and fragmentary. In other words, we can never fully know the other person as a unique individuality, nor can we know the other as an object with fixed, thing-like qualities. We have recourse, therefore, to 'thought experiments' and conceive of the other in interaction 'as being the human type which is suggested by his individuality'. We engage in typifications of individuals and groups, typifications which mediate between knowledge and action. The *second* apriori of individuality focuses upon the concept of the social role as the 'mediation of sociability and sociality' to the extent to which 'every element of a group is not only a societal part but, in addition, something else'. Here, Simmel seeks to guard against the 'oversocialized' concept of human beings as merely a bundle of roles. The individual is both a member, product and content of society, on the one hand, and an autonomous being who 'exists both for society and for himself'; an autonomous being which 'views his life from its own centre and for its own sake'. Human beings, as social animals

> are capable of constructing the notion of society from the very idea of beings, each of whom may feel himself as the *terminus a quo* and the *terminus ad quem* of his developments and destinies and qualities. And we do construct this concept of society, which is built up from that of the potentially autonomous individual, as the *terminus a quo* and the *terminus ad quem* of the individual's very life and fate. This capacity constitutes an apriori of empirical society. It makes possible the form of society as we know it. [33]

This 'form of society' brings us to the *third* apriori of society as 'a structure', as 'a web of qualitatively differentiated phenomena' that is, in fact, an 'ideal structure' within which

> The life of society (considered .... phenomenologically that is, exclusively in regard to its social contents) takes its course as if each of its elements were predestined for its particular place in it. In spite of all discrepancies between it and ideal standards, social life exists as if all of its elements found themselves interrelated with one another is such a manner that each of them, because of its very individuality, depends on all others and all others depend on it. [34]

Thus, 'social life presupposes an unquestionable harmony between the individual and society as a whole'. Were this harmony to reach perfection then it would produce 'not the *perfect* society, but the perfect *society*'. This third apriori is thus one of the ideational, logical presuppositions for the perfect society (which is perhaps never realized in this perfection, however)'. At the level of the individual, and anticipating Weber's development of the concept, 'empirical society becomes possible because of the apriori that finds its most obvious expression in the concept of vocation', conceived as 'the individualisation of the whole in the roles of the human subject'.

There is another important implication of Simmel's third apriori of society which anticipates a considerable amount of subsequent debate, not merely in relation to the study of society but also with regard to the methodological orientation of sociology itself. The 'dual nexus' of generality and individuality in social life has an important methodological implication for the study of society. As Simmel states it,

> *The nexus* by which each social element (each individual) is interwoven with the life and activities of every other, and *by which the external framework of society is produced, is a causal nexus. But it is transformed into a teleological nexus as soon as it is considered from the perspective of the elements that carry and produce it — individuals.* For they feel themselves to be egos whose behaviour grows out of autonomous, self-determined personalities. [35]

Not merely the possibility of society but also the possibility of reconciling explanation and understanding in relation to social life is highlighted by Simmel here, though whether what is at issue is merely a change in perspective must remain open to question.

It has been suggested that, in his discussion of the aprioris of society, Simmel comes closest to making 'the concept of "society" into a regulative idea of society and thus avoids from the outset the naive epistemological alternative of other theories of society, that from the start either dissolve society from the standpoint of the human subject or hypostatize it as objective' [36]. Simmel does seek to deal in this context with both a phenomenology of how 'society' is experienced and the heuristic transcendental presupposition of society as a regulative idea that ensures the unity of the object of society. However, Schrader-Klebert draws out the implications of Simmel's third apriori in a manner which goes beyond his own reflections. She argues that

> the self-foundation of sociology by means of the idea of society requires a concept of abstract utopia, a philosophical-historical premise. Then and only then can the idea of society fulfil its function as a critical concept, when its transcendentally grounded meaning is transformed into a postulate of practical reason; if its ... presupposition of a mediation of theory and practice is also still to be reflected in the results of knowledge; if its claim to know

reality also entails seeing through this reality; if its task is to be more than a description of what exists, then the object as the standard of critique must itself also imply a postulate for practice. [37]

No doubt this critical intention is present to some degree in Simmel's third apriori. But so also is his desire to limit the study of society to the study of sociation and thus possibly to separate out society as sociation from society as a transformable totality. At the end of his essay on 'How is society possible?', Simmel returns to his conception of sociology as the study of 'the variety of forms of interaction that constitute society', to a conception of sociological inquiry that is 'directed towards abstracting from the complex phenomenon called social life that which is purely society, that is, sociation. It eliminates from the purity of this concept everything which does not constitute society as a unique and autonomous form of existence, although it can be realized only historically in society' [38].

What does Simmel gain from this limitation of sociology to the study of forms of sociation and society to the synthesis of forms of interaction? It should be emphasized here that Simmel saw his sociology as concerned not with abstract forms of sociation but with their comparative and historical study. Simmel highlights social reality as a process of interaction between individuals whose study must presuppose not merely the agency of actors but also the examination of their motives, interests, and the unintended consequences of their interactions. But Simmel is not specifically concerned with individual actors as such, rather with the process of interaction between actors, since 'every social occurrence as such, consists of an interaction between individuals. In other words, each individual is at the same time an active and a passive agent in a transaction' [39] and one might add here Simmel is concerned with the reciprocal effects of actions. In this context, Simmel would certainly have readily concurred with Marx's notion of society as 'the product of human reciprocal action'. In a different context, Simmel might also see society as a complex of internal relations, within which any interaction could form the starting point of sociological inquiry.

The notion of social reality as the ceaseless interactions of its elements emphasizes not merely the processual nature of social reality but also its dynamic character. As Tenbruck suggests, 'since ... the forms of sociation are not viewed as variables of a given social system on which they are fundamentally dependent, society is not conceived of as an inert body seeking solely to maintain itself in the status quo' [40]. Simmel examines in his sociology the dynamic nature of these forms of sociation but not the dynamic of the whole. In this context, Tenbruck also pinpoints two aspects of sociology that have implications for the two conceptions of society with which Simmel originally commenced. For Simmel's sociology of forms of sociation,

> social change means tendencies in specific aspects of society. Formal sociology is incompetent to deal with the problem of a change of society itself, a change of the whole system. It cannot be otherwise, for it refuses to regard society, as conceived of as such a system, as its proper subject.
>
> On the other hand, as is well known, Simmel subscribed to broad theories of social change, that is, to theories of the long-term changes of social systems. [41]

In his later formulations of 'The Field of Sociology', 'the problem of how to account for the changes of society as a whole, is assigned to a branch of inquiry which borders on formal sociology, and into which it blends, namely, philosophical sociology or the philosophy of history'. [42]. In this distinctive sense, then, and setting a trend for much sociology in this century, society as a whole becomes an absent concept in the grounding of sociology.

We have examined Simmel's foundation of sociology in relation to the generation of a delimited concept of society in some detail because it not merely highlights the move towards the grounding of sociology without a concept of society as a whole, but because Simmel's sociology anticipates a wide range of traditions in the twentieth century which have advanced further along this path. A particular virtue of Simmel's deliberations is, however, that he still felt it necessary to reflect upon the implications of grounding sociology in a manner which did not take as its object society as a whole.

3.2 WEBER ON SOCIOLOGY AND SOCIAL ACTION

A brief examination of Max Weber's grounding of sociology, which has somewhat relatedly provided one of the most powerful traditions in modern sociology, will also confirm the tendency in sociology to abandon the concept of society as the starting point for the study of sociology. In his incomplete assessment of Simmel as a sociologist, Weber pointed to a crucial dimension of Simmel's sociology. Whereas many of those studying social life have been 'dealing with questions of "facticity", empirical questions, Simmel has turned to look at the "meaning" which we can obtain from the phenomenon (or can believe we can)' [43]. This meaning of social interaction, for instance, had been studied by Simmel through that process by which Weber was also to operate, namely through the construction of social types, the examination of the social scientist's typifications of participants in interaction and more generally, the interpretive understanding of actions' motivations. More significantly, however, Weber, writing over a decade after Simmel's early delineation of sociology, still detects that he himself is reflecting upon sociology within 'a period ... when sociologists who are to be taken very seriously maintain the thesis that the *only* task of sociological theory is the definition of the concept of society [44].

Weber's own grounding of sociology decisively breaks with such a thesis. Weber systematically avoids treating all collectivities and major social aggregates, of which society is one, as *sui generis* entities. Instead, they are all introduced as labels for tendencies towards action. Although one of his major works is entitled *Economy and Society*, it does not discuss 'the definition of the concept of society' but rather societal tendencies to action or sociation (*Vergesellschaftung*) which is contrasted with action motivated by a tendency towards solidarity and communality (*Vergemeinschaftung*). This becomes intelligible, as we shall see, in the light of Weber's definition of the subject-matter of sociology as the study of social action and its meaning for individual actors. The avoidance of the concept of society is justifiable for Weber given his commitment to the methodological individualist position. Such a commitment is most clearly evident in his statement that 'If I am now a sociologist ... I am so in order to put an end to the use of collective concepts, a use which still haunts us. In other words: even sociology can only start out from the action of one or a few, or many individuals i.e. pursue a strictly "individualistic" method' [45]. This is why Weber preferred to use verb forms or active nouns in order to delineate the social processes with which he was concerned. At all events, recourse to collective concepts by sociologists was only justified on the grounds that they referred to the actual or possible social actions of individuals. And this means, in contrast to Durkheim, that 'there is no such thing as a collective personality which "acts"'. Society cannot be the starting point of Weber's sociology.

Instead, Weber chose to emphasize the importance of individual actors, their agency, motivation and the meanings which can be imputed to their actions and those of others. Sociology is to be

a science concerning itself with the interpretive understanding of social action and thereby with a causal explanation of its course and consequences. We shall speak of 'action' insofar as the acting individual attaches a subjective meaning to his behavior — be it overt or covert, omission or acquiescence. Action is 'social' insofar as its subjective meaning takes account of the behaviour of others, and is thereby oriented in its course. [46]

In the light of the 'empirical uniformities' observable in social action and detected in 'courses of action that are repeated by the actor or (simultaneously) occur among numerous actors since the subjective meaning is meant to be the same', sociological investigation can move beyond the study of individual actions to 'typical modes of action' [47]. Sociology is thus a discipline which 'searches for empirical regularities and types' of human action. General sociology will thus attempt to 'systematically classify' social groups — formed, through concerted social action — according to the structure, content and means of social action' [48]. Hence, as well as elaborating a typology of social action — which 'ranges from mere consensual action (*Einverständnishandeln*) and ad hoc agreement (*Gelegenheitsvergesellschaftung*), through various kinds of regulated action and enduring association (*Vergesellschaftung*), to the organization (*Verband*) and compulsory institution (*Anstalt*)' [49] — sociology examines groups (*Gemeinschaften*) and group formation out of concerted social action. On one of the few occasions upon which Weber refers to society, he speaks of 'society' as 'the general structures of human groups' [50].

Society, however, like all other 'collective entities' is introduced in parentheses to indicate that not only is there, for sociological purposes, 'no such thing as a collective personality which "acts"' but also that our sociological reference to such entities implies '*only* a certain kind of development of actual or possible social actions of individual persons'. Such 'concepts of collective entities' — society, state, nation, family, etc. — are also to be found in 'common sense'. Indeed, insofar as they have meaning for individual actors, they can influence action itself. Collective concepts, such as society or state, do

have a meaning in the minds of individual persons, partly as of something actually existing, partly as something with normative authority ... Actors thus in part orient their action to them, and in this role *such ideas* have a powerful, often a decisive, causal influence on the course of action of real individuals. [52]

Such concepts, which actually signify 'a complex of social interaction of individual persons', thus have an additional significance for sociology insofar as actors orient their action towards them. But again, it should be emphasized that sociology is not directly concerned with such collectivities but with 'the subjective understanding of the action of the component individuals' which is 'the specific characteristic of sociological knowledge'. Sociology should examine, for instance, a particular community, and by implication, a society by asking the 'real empirical sociological' question:

> What motives determine and lead the individual members and participants in this ... community to behave in such a way that the community came into being in the first place and that it continues to exist? [53]

Weber is determined 'to avoid the "reification" of those concepts' which refer to collective forms of social organization.

But if sociology is to concern itself with the meanings and motives which individual actors attach to their actions, whether rationally formulated or not, then it must in some way have access to such meanings and motives through 'direct observational understanding' and 'explanatory understanding' which gives us access to 'intended meaning'. Sociology aims at the causal interpretation of the social action of individuals. It focuses upon such action as the 'subjectively understandable orientation of behaviour' and upon the motives for such action as 'a complex of subjective meaning which seems to the actor himself or to the observer an adequate ground for the conduct in question'. However, the typifications and meaning of social action might well be very different from the standpoint of 'the actor' and the 'observer'. It has often been pointed out that the 'subjective' and 'objective' meaning of social action and social relationships must be brought together more adequately than Weber was able to achieve. This has relevance, for example, for a conception of society as a complex of social relationships (which is not Weber's view). In this context, with regard to a social relationship, Weber again emphasized that

> it is *only* the existence of the probability that, corresponding to a given subjective meaning, a certain type of action will take place

which constitutes the 'existence' of the social relationship. Thus that a 'friendship' or a 'state' exists or has existed means this and only this: that we, the observers, judge that there is or has been a probability that on the basis of certain kinds of known subjective attitude of certain individuals there will result in the average sense a certain specific type of action. [54]

Not only is the absence of any ontological commitment to the existence of social realities evident here, but so too is the problematic of the judgement of the observers as the ultimate privileged source typifications of the social action of individual actors and of social relationships.

This problematic was systematically criticized by Alfred Schutz, whose phenomenological sociology takes as its starting point

not social action or social behavior, but *intentional conscious experiences directed towards the other self*. However, we include here only those intentional experiences which are related to the other *as other*, that is, as a conscious living being. [55]

In the light of this emphasis upon conscious, lived experience, Schutz is able to indicate that, with regard to Weber's definition of a social relationship, there exists 'two different kinds of situation' which establish the existence of a social relationship: 'the actor's subjective expectation' and 'the outside observer's "objective judgement"' [56]. This enables Schutz to argue that what sociology is doing, and especially what Weber's construction of ideal types of social action is doing, is creating 'objective meaning — contents of subjective meaning-contexts'. In his later works, Schutz examines more fully the typifications in the everyday world that are a necessary foundation for other typifications. And, however critical of Weber's interpretive sociology, Schutz remains committed to its focus upon individuals. For Schutz, interpretive sociology's 'primary task ... is to describe the processes of meaning-establishment and meaning-interpretation as these are carried out by individuals living in the social world' [57].

But if we return to Weber's sociological work and in particular to his impressive studies in historical sociology, it is clear that Weber does make one of the major contributions to the understanding of the development of modern Western rational societies. His 'developmental history' of modern society and its major economic, political, legal, religious and social institutions is made possible through the construction of ideal types of economic formation, system of legitimation and so on. On the basis of his distinctive notion of concept formation, Weber is interested in 'the specific cultural significance' of any of these social institutions and forms of social activity. Indeed, if Weber does systematically seek to avoid the concept of society, the same cannot be said of culture, viewed as 'a finite segment of the meaningless infinity of the world process, a segment which from the point of view of *human beings* has meaning and significance conferred upon it'. The ideal type (of capitalism, form of legitimation, etc.) is 'a purely ideal *limiting* concept for the *comparison* with and *scrutiny* of reality for the purpose of emphasizing certain significant parts of empirical reality' [58]. If at times, Weber seems concerned to develop sociology as a science of culture (*Kulturwissenschaft*), then his methodology prompts him to focus on what is significant out of the infinity of possible cultural objects of study.

The importance of cultural phenomena as part of sociology's object-domain is emphasized by Weber and by Simmel. Since they are both concerned with the developmental tendencies in modern society, they are both, despite their restriction of the tasks of sociology, committed to the development of theories of society, perhaps transposed onto the level of philosophies of history. Simmel's theory of the growing alienation of objective culture from the subjective culture of individuals and Weber's problematic of the progressive rationalization of the social and natural world are both instances of this [59]. Is there a tendency for a sociology that confines itself to the study of social interaction or social action to develop overarching theories of society that seek to take account of the absent parameter of society in the theory of social action? [60]. Certainly these sociologies do generate theories of societal or historical tendencies that threatened the existence of the very individuals which the more restricted sociological programmes sought to take as their starting point.

REFERENCES

[1] H.-J. Dahme, 'Der Verlust des Fortschrittsglaubens und die Verwissenschaftlichung der Soziologie. Ein Vergleich von Simmel, Tönnies und Weber', unpublished paper, Bielefeld, 1984.

[2] G. Simmel, *Über sociale Differenzierung*, Leipzig, Duncker & Humblot, 1890, p. 9.

[3] G. Simmel, 'Das Problem der Soziologie', *Jahrbuch für Gesetzgebung, Verwaltung und Volkswirtshaft*, 18, 1984, p. 277.

[4] G. Simmel, *Über sociale Differenzierung*, op. cit., p. 13.

[5] Ibid., p. 15.

[6] Ibid., p. 10.

[7] G. Simmel, 'Die Selbsterhaltung der sozialen Gruppe', *Jahrbuch für Gesetzgebung, Verwaltung und Volkswirtschaft*, **22**, 1898, p. 235.

[8] G. Simmel, 'The Problem of Sociology', *Annals of the American Academy of Political and Social Science*, **6**, 1895, pp. 415–416.

[9] G. Simmel, 'Das Problem der Soziologie', *op. cit.*, p. 275.

[10] G. Simmel, 'The Problem of Sociology', *op. cit.*, pp. 421–422.

[11] G. Simmel, 'Superiority and Subordination as Subject-Matter of Sociology', *American Journal of Sociology*, **2**, 1896, p. 167.

[12] G. Simmel, 'Massenpsychologie', *Die Zeit* (Vienna), **5**, 23.11.1895.

[13] G. Simmel, 'Zur Methodik der Sozialwissenschaften', *Jahrbuch für Gesetzgebung, Verwaltung und Volkswirtschaft*, **20**, 1896, pp. 232–233.

[14] Ibid., p. 233.

[15] G. Simmel, 'Die Selbsterhaltung der sozialen Gruppen', op. cit., p. 238.

[16] G. Simmel, *The Philosophy of Money* (trans. T. Bottomore and D. Frisby), London and Boston, Routledge, 1978, p. 101.

[17] G. Simmel, 'The Problem of Sociology', op. cit., pp. 422–423.

[18] Ibid., pp. 421–422.

[19] G. Simmel, 'Superiority and Subordination', op. cit., p. 167.

[20] Ibid., p. 168.

[21] G. Simmel, 'Soziologie der Sinne', *Neue Rundschau*, **18**, 1907, p. 1025.

[22] G. Simmel, 'The Problem of Sociology', in K. H. Wolff (ed.), *Essays on Sociology, Philosophy and Aesthetics by Georg Simmel, et al.*, Columbus, Ohio, Ohio University Press, 1959, p. 327. Our emphasis.

[23] G. Simmel, 'Sozioligie der Sinne', op. cit., p. 1026. Our emphasis.

[24] Ibid., p. 1035.

[25] G. Simmel, 'Superiority and Subordination', op. cit., p. 169.

[26] D. Levine (ed.), *Georg Simmel on Individuality and Social Forms*, Chicago, University of Chicago Press, 1971, p. 129.

[27] Ibid., p. 134.

[28] G. Simmel, *The Philosophy of Money*, op. cit., p. 174.

[29] K. H. Wolff (ed.), *Essays on Sociology, Philosophy and Aesthetics*, op. cit., p. 340.

[30] Ibid., pp. 339–340.

[31] Ibid., p. 341.

[32] U. Gerhardt, *Rollenanalyse als kritische Soziologie*, Neuwied and Berlin, Luchterhand, 1971, pp. 27–40.

[33] K. H. Wolff (ed.), *Essays on Sociology, Philosophy and Aesthetics*, op. cit., p. 351.

[34] Ibid., p. 353.

[35] Ibid., p. 355. Our emphasis.
[36] K. Schrader-Klebert, 'Der Begriff der Gesellschaft als regulative Idee', *Soziale Welt*, **19**, 1968, p. 105.
[37] Ibid., p. 116.
[38] K. H. Wolff (ed.), *Essays on Sociology, Philosophy and Aesthetics*, op. cit., pp. 355–356.
[39] G. Simmel, 'Superiority and Inferiority', op. cit., p. 169.
[40] F. Tenbruck, 'Formal Sociology', in K. H. Wolff (ed.), *op. cit.*, p. 89.
[41] Ibid., p. 90.
[42] Ibid., pp. 90–91.
[43] M. Weber, 'Georg Simmel as Sociologist', *Social Research*, **39**, 1972, p. 161.
[44] Ibid., pp. 161–162.
[45] O. Stammer (ed.), *Max Weber and Sociology Today*, Oxford, Blackwell, 1971, p. 115.
[46] M. Weber, *Economy and Society* (ed. G. Roth and C. Wittich), Berkeley, Los Angeles and London, University of California Press, 1978, p. 4.
[47] Ibid., p. 29.
[48] Ibid., p. 356.
[49] Ibid., p. lxviii.
[50] Ibid., p. 356.
[51] Ibid., p. 14.
[52] Ibid., p. 14. Our emphasis.
[53] Ibid., p.18.
[54] Ibid., p. 28.
[55] A. Schutz, *The Phenomenology of the Social World* (trans. G. Walsh and F. Lenhert), Evanston, Northwestern University Press, 1967, p. 144.
[56] Ibid., p. 152.
[57] Ibid., p. 248.
[58] Cited in T. Burger, *Max Weber's Theory of Concept Formation*, Durham, North Carolina, Duke University Press, 1976.
[59] See G. Simmel, *The Philosophy of Money*, op. cit., esp. ch. 6. For Weber, see the careful study of R. Brubaker, *The Limits of Rationality*, London, Allen & Unwin, 1984.
[60] This is one of the implications that can be drawn from Alan Dawe's argument on 'The Two Sociologies'. See, most recently, A. Dawe, 'Theories of Social Action', in T. Bottomore and R. Nisbet (eds.), *A History of Sociological Analysis*, London, Heinemann, New York, Basic Books, 1978.

4

Society as idea and ideal

The notion of society as idea and ideal which we wish to discuss in this chapter is developed in various traditions, which are in other respects often opposed to one another. We shall exemplify such perspectives, rather than in any way treat them exhaustively, here. In this conception, the problem of meaning is acknowledged as central to sociology, but individualist modes of analysis of meaning of the sort encountered in the last chapter are rejected as inadequate. Instead, meaning is seen as inherently and necessarily a *social* phenomenon, something always presupposed to individual action in the way that a language is presupposed to any particular utterance. Society itself is accordingly apprehended as the network of shared understandings, the cognitive and communicative community which makes the actions of individuals — a prayer, a promise, a vote — meaningful to themselves and others. Society, in this perspective, is ideal in the German philosophic sense: it *is* a reality, not a mere absent concept, whose existence must be conceded if the meaningfulness of individual action is itself to be comprehensible. But this reality is not — or at least not exclusively — a material one.

4.1 DURKHEIM REVISITED: *REPRÉSENTATIONS COLLECTIVES*

One, neglected source of this view of society as ideal lies, somewhat paradoxically, in Durkheim, a pioneer here as elsewhere. Durkheim is often, and with justification, criticized for his neglect of the problem of meaning. In *Suicide*, for example, in pursuit of the objective stance discussed in Chapter 2, he attempts entirely (and notoriously) to abstract from individual suicides' intentionality, explaining variations in suicide rates by social factors alone. But Durkheim's thought is complex, and difficult to pigeonhole into neat categories — positivist, naturalist, and so on. His later writings develop what is at its strongest a definition of society in terms of meaning, although meaning is not conceived with primary reference to the individual as it is for Simmel or Weber. Hence the sui generis postulate is preserved, even while the irreducibly meaningful, 'ideal' character of social phenomena is acknowledged.

Central to Durkheim's later work is the concept of what he called *représentations collectives* — collective representations, or symbols. 'In social life', he writes, 'everything consists of representations, ideas and sentiments'; 'society is a complex of ideas and sentiments, of ways of seeing and of feeling, a certain intellectual and moral framework distinctive of the entire group. Society is above all a consciousness of the whole'. Indeed at one point Durkheim goes so far as to say that society is 'above all the idea which it forms of itself' [1]. We saw in Chapter 2 that society for Durkheim is a moral order. Here it emerges that society is equally for him a *cognitive* order. Society furnishes not merely the content of our thought — our specific beliefs and sentiments — but (a much more radical thesis) provides the very mental framework *in* which we think.

This aspect of Durkheim's concept of society is developed most fully — indeed messianically — in *Primitive Classification* (with Marcel Mauss, 1903 [2]) and *Elementary Forms of the Religious Life*. Here, Durkheim ascribes a social origin both to logical thought in general and specifically to the philosophers' categories of the understanding — the concepts of space, time, relation, cause, number, and so on, through which all subjective, individual experience is ordered. This is one of his boldest theories, proposing nothing less than a sociological solution to the age-old philosophical problem of knowledge. It remains highly controversial. Nonetheless it is, in our view, an extremely fruitful line of argument with respect to the concept of society, whether or not one ultimately accepts Durkheim's epistemological claims as such.

Logical thought, Durkheim argues, is made up of concepts. Concepts are distinguished from the sensations of individuals, first, by their stability, and second, by what Durkheim refers to as their universality or impersonality. The sensations of individual experience 'are in a perpetual flux', they are 'fugitive conceptions'. Concepts, by contrast, are 'as it were, outside of time and change [. . .] It is a manner of thinking that, at every moment in time, is fixed and crystallized' [3]. This does not mean concepts do not alter historically — for Durkheim they emphatically do — but that they are immutable from the point of view of the individual. They are objective, in the sense elucidated in Chapter 2; though entirely mental, they nonetheless share with material things the characteristic of not being modifiable by an act of individual will. And where sensations are personal, 'the concept is universal, or at least capable of becoming so. A concept is not my concept; I hold it in common with other men, or, in any case, can communicate it to them [. . .] The concept is an essentially impersonal representation; it is through it that human intelligences communicate' [4]. Durkheim draws a not unexpected conclusion from this:

> The nature of the concept, thus defined, bespeaks its origin. If it is common to all, it is the work of the community [. . .] it is unquestionable that language, and consequently the system of concepts which it translates, is the product of a collective elaboration. What it expresses is the manner in which society as a whole represents the facts of experience. [5]

Durkheim's argument here — once again — is that this social fact, language, could not have arisen out of individual actions, for they always presuppose it. Concepts are not social because they are general among individuals, they are general among individuals because their origin is social. Concepts are born in the sui generis collectivity itself, and imposed, by the action of society, on individuals. For Durkheim, their characteristics are such — are so far removed from what pertains to individual sensation and experience — that they cannot begin to be explained otherwise. There is nothing in individual experience which could give rise to conceptual thought:

> It is under the form of collective thought that impersonal thought is for the first time revealed to humanity; we cannot see by what other way this revelation could have been made. From the mere fact that society exists, there is also, outside of the individual sensations and images, a whole system of representations which enjoy marvellous properties. By means of them, men understand each other and intelligences grasp each other. They have within them a sort of force or moral ascendency, in virtue of which they impose themselves upon individual minds. [6]

What Durkheim argues here for concepts in general applies with added force to the categories of the understanding, the very scaffold without which no logical thought is possible. Traditional epistemology had thrown up two broad answers to the problem of the origin of the categories. The Humean empiricist tradition saw them as arising cumulatively out of individual sensory experience, while the Kantian tradition held them to be logically prior to the very possibility of experience, and therefore innate in the human mind. Durkheim attempted to transcend the dichotomy by arguing that the categories were, indeed, prior to and irreducible to individual experience, but originated in (and changed with) *society* rather than being innate in the mind. Kant was right, in Durkheim's view, to reject an individualist, sensory account of the origin of the categories — their transcendent stability and universality spoke against it. But the hypothesis of innateness, for him, is irreconcilable with the manifest historical variation in the specific content of these categories, and merely begs the question which a sociological epistemology answers.

Only society, Durkheim argues, has the requisite authority — the transcendent moral power, deriving from its sui generis nature, discussed in Chapter 2 — to impose such eminently collective concepts. The two defining features of the categories — their universality and necessity – corresponds exactly to the two defining characteristics of all social facts, generality and constraint, and 'almost necessarily implies that they be of social origin' [7]. It should not surprise us by now to find that he specifically roots the categories in religion (entailing the paradox, which Durkheim evidently delights in, that scientific thought is of religious origin). The authority of reason itself, for Durkheim, is thus

> the very authority of society, transferring itself to a certain manner of thought which is the indispensable condition of all common action. The necessity with which the categories are imposed upon us is not the effect of simple habits whose yoke we could easily throw off with a little effort; nor is it a physical or metaphysical necessity, since the categories change in different places and times; it is a special sort of moral necessity which is to the intellectual life what moral obligation is to the will. [8]

Beyond this, Durkheim also advanced the more specific claim that society is not only the source of, but itself the model for, the categories. 'They not only come from society, but the things which they express are of a social nature' [9]. The category of class is founded on that of the human group, that of time on the rhythms of collective life — particularly those of religious ceremonial — that of space on tribal territory, that of cause on the collective force of society itself. And the most abstract and general of all categories, the concept of totality, is 'only the most abstract from of the concept of society: it is the whole which includes all things, the supreme class which embraces all other classes' [10]. Durkheim adds, characteristically: 'at bottom, the concept of totality, that of society, and that of divinity are very probably aspects of the same notion' [11]. Interestingly Karl Marx had anticipated this line of argument, seventy years previously, opining that 'my general consciousness is only the *theoretical* shape of that of which the living shape is the *real* community, the social fabric' [12].

Whatever the adequacy of these claims as epistemology, Durkheim touches here on what must undoubtedly be a fundamental dimension of any worthwhile concept of society. Society is — irrespective of any other characteristics it might possess — a communicative community, a symbolic order, a universe of shared (or at the least, of intercommunicable) meanings. Now this is interesting, because a concern with meaning is central to the mainly anti-Durkheimian sociologies we considered in the last chapter. These sociologies are united by their reference to individuals and their action, and an implicit or explicit rejection of the concept of society as such. The question Durkheim's analysis of *représentations collectives* forcefully raises, however, is whether the meaningfulness of individual action can be intelligibly analysed at all without presupposing a society which has at least some of the sui generis characteristics he ascribes to it. His sociological rewrite of Kant accepts the Kantian denial of the possibility of the categories of the understanding arising out of individual experience alone, and therefore sees meaning as presupposed to individual action. The social fact, language, is presupposed to — and is therefore not explicable simply as the sum of — individual speech-acts. For Durkheim, in short, it is only the reality of a transcendent, albeit ideal society which makes meaningful individual actions possible at all. Others, to whom we shall now turn, have reached similar conclusions by rather different routes.

4.2 WINCH: SOCIETY AS IDEA

A not dissimilar line of argument, which explicitly rejects the standpoint of Durkheim the 'positivist', has been advanced by Peter Winch in his *The Idea of a Social Science* (1958). Winch's plea for a sociology devoted to interpretive understanding in order to do justice to the distinctive nature of social phenomena appears, at first sight, to be remarkably close to Weber's emphasis upon sociology as the study of the meaningful behaviour of social actors. But not only does Winch outline some correctives to Weber's concept of understanding, he also commences from a very different starting point, namely Ludwig Wittgenstein's reflections upon the nature of language games, rule following and forms of life, especially in his *Philosophical Investigations* (1953). In so doing, and despite the extensive criticism advanced against many of Winch's arguments, 'he succeeds in calling attention to a number of complex issues that must be confronted in any adequate theorizing about society — issues which are played down or suppressed by mainstream social scientists' [13].

Winch applies Wittgenstein's insights into the nature of language, its dependency upon rule-following and the relationship between language games and forms of life to questions concerning the nature of social phenomena, our conceptualization of them and the possibility of understanding meaningful behaviour. For Winch, 'the problem of what language is is clearly of vital importance for sociology in that, with it, one is face to face with the whole question of the characteristic way in which human beings interact with each other in society' [14]. For example, language conditions how we see and experience the reality of society, insofar as

> Our idea of what belongs to the realm of reality is given for us in the language that we use. The concepts we have settle for us the form of experience we have of the world . . . The world *is* for us what is presented through those concepts. [15]

Our elucidation of these concepts is an elucidation of that to which they refer: 'For example, the question of what constitutes social behaviour is a demand for an elucidation of the concept of social behaviour' [16]. Central to what takes place in human society and central to its investigation by sociology is therefore the understanding and interpretation of social relations and conceptions of social relations.

Here we approach the heart of Winch's conception of society and his notion of sociology committed to interpretive understanding. Against Durkheim's early rejection of 'the notions of those who participate' in society as a source of explanation or interpretation of social life, Winch advances the thesis that 'a Man's social relations with his fellows are permeated with his ideas about reality. Indeed, 'permeated' is hardly a strong enough word: *social relations are expressions of ideas about reality'* [17]. Their study is not to be undertaken on the basis of methodological individualism. Rather, it 'involves a consideration of the general nature of a human society, an analysis, that is, of the concept of a human society.'

Drawing upon Wittgenstein's insights into 'rule-following' in language games, Winch seeks to show 'the way in which the epistemological discussion of man's understanding of reality throws light on the nature of human society and of social relations between men' [18]. The meaning of words, the 'sameness' of their meaning is inextricably bound up with the act of rule following. The principle of rule following is not merely crucial for language games but also for the understanding of human behaviour. Rule following, like language, is inherently social. In examining whether a person's behaviour is following a rule we must take account,

> not only of the the actions of the person whose behaviour is in

question as a candidate for the category of rule-following, but also the *reactions* of other people to what he does. More specifically, it is only in a situation in which it makes sense to suppose that somebody else could in principle discover the rule which I am following that I can intelligibly be said to follow a rule at all. [19]

A second criterion for rule-following is that 'the notion of following a rule is logically inseparable from the notion of *making a mistake*'. In turn, this depends upon the property of 'making a mistake' which is 'a contravention of what is established as correct; as such, it must be *recognizable* as such a contravention' [20]. Again, 'the necessity for rules to have a social setting' is verified by the notion of establishing a standard which is not an activity ascribable 'to any individual in complete isolation from other individuals'. From this it follows that it is meaningless 'to suppose anyone capable of establishing a purely personal standard of behaviour *if* he had never had any experience of human society with its socially established rules' [21]. Furthermore, the whole notion of the meaning of rules, utterances, etc., is located in society: the 'very categories of meaning, etc., are *logically* dependent for their sense on social interaction between men'; indeed, 'the very existence of concepts depends on group life' [22].

Winch's 'correction' of Weber's starting point for sociology is thus that 'all meaningful behaviour must be social, since it can be meaningful only if governed by rules, and rules presuppose a social setting' [23]. It implies the extension of meaningful behaviour beyond that for which the agent has a 'reason' to those instances in which the application of a rule can be demonstrated. It also implies that reflection upon rules can take place in the sense that 'understanding something involves understanding the contradictory too' (enabling action orientated against established rules).

If we have outlined some of the implications of Winch's emphasis upon the identity of ideas and social relations for the grounding of sociology as the interpretation of meaningful social behaviour, what are the implications for the study of society? In other words, what follows from Winch's view that 'the social relations between men and the ideas which men's actions embody are really the same thing considered from different points of view' [24] for our understanding of society? The simplest answer to this question is that society is a set of internal relations, just as language is also a set of internal relations. Taking the realm of language first, we can see that Winch views language's expression in concepts and discourse as entailing the existence of a language-game with the parameters of a system. Thus, 'the relation between idea and context is an *internal* one. The idea gets its sense from the role it plays in the system' [25]. The context of an idea is how it belongs 'in a certain way to a system of ideas'. The same holds for 'the realm of discourse and . . . the internal relations that link the parts of a realm of discourse' [26].

However, since the meaning of ideas (and a discourse) is merely the description of their usage and since to describe how they are used is to describe the social intercourse into which they enter, so 'our language and our social relations are just two different sides of the same coin'. Therefore, 'if social relations between men exist only in and through their ideas, then, since the relations between ideas are internal relations, social relations must be a species of internal relations too' [27]. This should not be understood in a totally static manner since 'a new way of talking sufficiently important to rank as a new idea implies a new set of social relationships' [28]. The idea of civil society, for instance, implies a new set of social relationships that are that civil society. The internal relations between ideas are dependent upon internal relations in society. The latter share the same property as the former, so that 'it will seem less strange that social relations should be like logical relations between propositions once it is seen that logical relations between propositions themselves depend on social relations between men' [29]. If we accept this, then social interaction itself 'can more profitably be compared to the exchange of ideas in a conversation than to the interaction of forces in a physical system' [30]. The system of social relations that is society can then be viewed as a system of discourses. Life within society 'is carried on in terms of symbolic ideas which express certain attitudes as between man and man' [31], in terms of 'symbolic relationships' that crucially affect merely 'material' ones.

Society as a 'form of life', is, then, a system of internal relations that exist through ideas about those relations. Winch's standpoint admits of social change in society and its investigation by historical research. The latter appears akin to a history of discourse, though not necessarily, for instance, in Foucault's sense. This can be seen from the following summary of many of Winch's arguments; commencing from the proposition that

> social relations really exist only in and through the ideas which are current in society; or alternatively, that social relations fall into the same logical category as do relations between ideas. It follows that social relations must be an equally unsuitable subject for generalizations and theories of the scientific sort to be formulated about them. Historical explanation is not the application of generalizations and theories to particular instances: it is the tracing of internal relations. It is like applying one's knowledge of a language in order to understand a conversation . . . Non-linguistic behaviour, for example, has an 'idiom' in the same kind of way as has a language. [32]

Translated into Wittgenstein's terminology, what Winch is arguing is that society as a language-game is dependent upon society as a form of life and vice versa. What sociologists are doing in interpreting forms of life is only possible through their interpretation of the language games associated with the form of life. In a different context, this might illuminate those sociological practices which take as their starting point the elucidation of members of society's common-sense accounts of social relations and society through the routine practices by which members make social situations and society meaningful. In a practical sense, they investigate meaning as usage in Wittgenstein's sense [33].

With regard to a theory of society, Winch's emphasis upon the internal relations of the language-game and society, as a form of life, as a set of internal relations, has the advantage of escaping the methodological individualism of earlier theories of social meaning. Now meaning in society is located intersubjectively through the medium of language. And although society is conceived as an ideational constellation of internal relations, this again is an advance on a conception of society as a summation of individuals or individual meanings. What Winch's conception fails to unlock is the constitution of the forms of life on which language games depend. To do this, he would have to examine the material relations of the language game and generate a conception of sociology that was concerned with more than the interpretation of meaningful social action.

4.3 CRITICAL THEORY: SOCIETY AS TRANSCENDENTAL IDEAL

One of the commonest criticisms of Winch's position has been that outside the parameters of language games there exist no criteria for comparison of language games themselves and for truth and falsity. This criticism has been raised in connection with the possibility of understanding other societies/language games and the status of that understanding [34]. This problem is related to the conception of the boundary of society as the boundary of its language-game. But whereas most critics have hastily rejected Winch's position as both idealist and relativist, others have adopted a more sympathetic critical position. And amongst the latter should be numbered the critical theorists, Karl-Otto Apel and Jürgen Habermas. It should, of course, be emphasized here that what follows is only a small part, however significant, of the critical theory project that does not take account of its earlier tradition associated with Max Horkheimer, Theodor Adorno, Herbert Marcuse and others [35].

Apel, for instance, sees the notion of participation in a language game as opening up the 'transcendence of the subject–object separation which can only be meaningfully required for the interpretative human or social sciences' [36] in opposition to their positivistic and objectivistic traditions. Drawing on Winch's later writings, in which he recognizes the normative parameters for intersubjective agreement within a language game, Apel agrees with Winch that, for instance, 'the norm of truthful discourse is . . . a precondition for the possibility of any functioning language-game and must therefore not merely be accepted in principle in any society but, to a certain degree, must be fulfilled in order for communication to be possible at all'. Similarly, '"integrity" is an indispensable presupposition for the functioning of social institutions (for role behaviour) in the same sense, as "fair play" is indispensable for the possibility of games' [37].

The recognition of such normative preconditions for the possibility of a language-game and a form of life bring Winch's position closer to that of recent critical theory which has come to examine the counterfactual ideal presuppositions of communication in society. Thus, for Apel, Winch's later position 'points to the both hermeneutically and ethically . . . relevant norms of the ideal language-game that we must presuppose — even though imperfectly realised or marred by socially-specific malformations — in any language-game and that means in any human form of life' [38]. This includes, of course, the language games of social scientists and their object (other human beings). To translate this problem of intersubjective understanding into a wider context, the 'scientific' language-game of the social scientist can only interpret the 'everyday' language-game of other human beings, not by the translation of the former into the latter or vice versa, but by the presupposition of 'an already presupposed understanding between language-games (of the social scientist and his objects) [39]. The presupposition of the transcendental language-game — the 'ideal unity of understanding that each person, who himself speaks or who listens to another, has always already made' — in turn makes possible the presupposition that 'any "language-game" as a *language-*game (and this means, any *human* form of life) is capable of being transcended and expanded by *self-reflection* through philosophy or critical social science' [40].

In order for this self-reflection to take place, in the context of the 'interwoven' nature of actions and linguistic usage that secures the internal relations between actions and concepts, Apel proposes

> to interpret the 'interwovenness' of linguistic usage, activity, expression of life and interpretation of the world in Wittgenstein's 'language-games' or 'forms of life' in terms of a *dialectical unity* that does not exclude *contradiction* between its *elements*. In my opinion, it is only given this proviso that talk of 'internal relations'

is transferable from logico-mathematical systems to 'given' social circumstances of life. [41]

Such a proposition has two implications. Firstly, with regard to the 'internal relations' that we 'take human actions and words seriously *hermeneutically* in terms of their potential intelligibility and even truth or normative and ethical correctness in the context of an ideal language-game with *internal relations* between words and actions (and knowledge)' [42]. Secondly, however, we must recognize that within given language-games and existing forms of life, discrepancies and contradictions between concepts and actions exist that must also be rendered intelligible by the analysis of the external relations 'between unconscious ideas and constrained modes of behaviour or between interests that are immanent to practice (i.e. meaningful motives that are not conceptually explicated) and official linguistic regulations *qua* "institutional fictions"' [43]. Thus, it is not only possible but necessary to transcend and subject to critique systematically distorted language-games. This is achieved through a distinctive

combination of quasi-causal explanation and deep-hermeneutic understanding (especially of unconscious teleological behaviour) that extends beyond actual linguistic usage and actual self-understanding of social forms of life, which characterizes the *methodological* procedures of the *critique of ideology*. [44]

The critique of ideology does not, like Wittgenstein's philosophy, leave the world as it is but engages in a 'critique of whole forms of life and their official language games'. However, 'his goal . . . can be achieved in the long run only with the practical realization of the unlimited communication community in the language-games of social systems of self-assertion' [45]. In other words, until that practical realization takes place, the possibility of 'the unlimited communication community' or Habermas's 'domination-free discourse' must be presupposed from the outset as a transcendental ideal, especially in the face of 'systematically distorted communication' in existing societies.

This hermeneutic–dialectical version of dealing with society as a subject –object of science presupposes that 'the concepts that are to be applied in the social sciences must, *in principle,* be capable of being used by the objects *qua* possible subjects of science for their own self-understanding' [46]. It follows from this, however, that those engaging in such sciences must presuppose an 'unlimited ideal communication community' that, through 'domination-free discourse', is able to achieve a consensus. But the parameters of this transcendentally presupposed ideal community (society), must extend beyond the scientific community since the social scientist is not merely observer but participant in the language-game that is to be investigated. Hence it is the case that

> Since this participation is ultimately made possibly by the fact that the subject–object of the social sciences is, in principle, capable of following rules that have been reflected upon (to a certain extent, capable of meta-communication), the ideal communication community as the precondition for the possibility of reaching scientific consensus, must ultimately incorporate society as the subject–object of science. [47]

The ideal communication community is thus the ideal domination-free society. Participation in the actual language-game presupposes the ideal language-game of unlimited communication and discourse. This counterfactual presupposition retains the possibility of the ideal society.

Yet the social sciences, and sociology in particular, are not merely concerned with language games conceived as static entities. Sociology, for Habermas, is certainly concerned with language — and with its importance not merely for the reasons outlined by Apel above but also its transmission in tradition, its historical dimension so weakly dealt with by Winch — but also with labour and domination. We can redraw the connection between language and domination hinted at in Apel's presentation. As Habermas argues,

> It makes good sense to conceive of language as a kind of metainstitution on which all social institutions are dependent; for social action is constituted only in ordinary language communication. But this metainstitution of language as tradition is evidently dependent in turn on social processes that are not exhausted in normative relationships. Language is *also* a medium of domination and social power. It serves to legitimate relations of organized force. Insofar as the legitimations do not articulate the relations of force that they make possible, insofar as these relations are merely expressed in legitimations, language is also ideological. Here it is not a question of deceptions within a language, but of deception with language as such. [48]

Society, social relations, social action and cultural tradition cannot, therefore, be reduced to sets of internal relations within language games any more than sociological investigation can be reduced to the elucidation and explication of meaning. The parameters of social relations and social action are not confined to the boundaries of language-games. For this reason,

> The objective framework within which social action can be comprehended without surrendering its intentionality is not merely a web of transmitted meanings and linguistically articulated tradition. The dimensions of labour and domination cannot be suppressed in favour of subjectively intended symbolic contents. A functionalist framework can also give non-normative conditions their due. Cultural tradition then loses the appearance of an absolute that a self-sufficient hermeneutics falsely lends to it. Tradition *as a whole* can be assigned its place; it can be conceived in its relation to the systems of social labour and political domination. [49]

The functionalist framework of which Habermas speaks here — though containing echoes of an insufficiently reflected Marxism — is intended to be one that is historically oriented, one that 'does not aim at technically useful information; it is guided by an emancipatory cognitive interest that aims only at reflection and demands enlightenment about one's own formative process' [50].

Habermas's emancipatory cognitive interest guiding a critical theory of society seems, in the context of a functionalist framework, to be a merely formal interest. Yet, for Habermas it is both substantive and normative. In this respect, Habermas follows the earlier Franfurt School tradition in studying society not merely as it exists but in terms of what that society contains as an anticipation of the future. In the present context, we can see that although Habermas might still view society as an emergent totality, as, in the Hegelian sense, in the process of 'becoming', what is both presupposed and anticipated in Habermas's later work is the 'ideal speech situation', the 'domination on free discourse' of a society grounded in emancipation and enlightenment. The ideal speech situation, in which there is a consensus concerning the validity of that which is necessary for communication to take place, can only be anticipated in actual communication within existing societies. It presupposes, of course, an ideal community or society within which unrestrained communication and discourse can take place. As McCarthy has argued,

> the analysis of the ideal speech situation shows it to involve assumptions about the context of interaction in which speech is located. The end result of this chain of argument is that the very structure of speech involves the anticipation of a form of life in

which autonomy and responsibility are possible. 'The critical theory of society takes this as its point of departure'. Its normative foundation is therefore not arbitrary, but inherent in the very structure of social action which it analyzes. [51]

This presupposed and anticipated society as ideal is one that is the result not merely of the process of emancipation but also of enlightenment [52]. Unlike the earlier tradition of the Frankfurt School, and especially its classic programmatic statements by Horkheimer and others [53], Habermas does not rely upon Marx's critique of political economy as the only model for the analysis of society. And although, against all neopositivist conceptions of piecemeal social engineering as the goal of social science [54], he remains committed to the possibility of the analysis of society as a totality, this totality cannot be simply inferred from an uncritical recourse to Marx's writings. Indeed, Habermas's recent work [55] has moved in the direction of a more comprehensive theory of social action that seeks to develop a theory of communicative action.

REFERENCES

[1] 'The method of sociology', *The Rules of Sociological Method,* ed. S. Lukes, London, Macmillan, 1982, p. 247; *Moral Education,* qutoed in introduction to R. N. Bellah (ed.), *Emile Durkheim on Morality and Society,* Chicago, Chicago University Press, 1973, p. xlii; *The Elementary Forms of the Religious Life,* ed. R. Nisbet, London, Allen & Unwin, 1976, p. 422.

[2] E. Durkheim and M. Mauss, *Primitive Classification,* London, Cohen & West, 1963.

[3] *Elementary forms,* p. 433.

[4] Ibid.

[5] Ibid., p. 434.

[6] Ibid., pp. 436–437.

[7] Ibid., pp. 17–18.

[8] Ibid.

[9] Ibid., p. 440.

[10] Ibid., p. 442.

[11] Ibid., p. 442n.

[12] K. Marx, Economic and philosophic manuscripts of 1844, in *Collected Works,* vol. 3, London, Lawrence & Wishart 1975, p. 298. 'But what would old Hegel say if he heard in the next world that the *general* [das *Allgemeine*] in German and Norse means nothing but the common land, and the particular [ds *Sundre, Besondre*] — nothing but the

separate property divided off from the common land? The logical categories are in that case damn well arising out of "our intercourse"'. Letter to 3ngles, 25 February 1868, in *Selected Correspondence,* Moscow, 1975.

[13] R. J. Bernstein, *The Restructuring of Social and Political Theory,* Oxford, Blackwell, 1976, pp. 64–65.

[14] P. Winch, *The Idea of a Social Science,* London, Routledge, 1958, p. 43.

[15] Ibid., p. 15.

[16] Ibid., p. 18.

[17] Ibid., p. 23. Our emphasis.

[18] Ibid., p. 24.

[19] Ibid., p. 30.

[20] Ibid., p. 32.

[21] Ibid., p. 33.

[22] Ibid., p. 44.

[23] Ibid., p. 116.

[24] Ibid., p. 10.

[25] Ibid., p. 107.

[26] Ibid., p. 115.

[27] Ibid., p. 123.

[28] Ibid., p. 122–123.

[29] Ibid., p. 126.

[30] Ibid., p. 128.

[31] Ibid., p. 131.

[32] Ibid., p. 133.

[33] For an introduction to this ethnomethodological tradition, see: D. Benson and J. A. Hughes, *The Perspective of Ethnomethodology,* London and New York, Longman, 1983; A. V. Cicourel, *Cognitive Sociology,* Harmondsworth, Penguin, 1973; H. Garfinkel, *Studies in Ethnomethodology,* Englewood Cliffs, N. J., Prentice-Hall, 1967.

[34] Some of these criticisms are contained in B. Wilson (ed.), *Rationality,* Oxford, Blackwell, 1970.

[35] For an introduction to this tradition, see M. Jay, *Dialectical Imagination,* Boston and Toronto, Little, Brown & Co., 1973.

[36] K. O. Apel, *Towards a Transformation of Philosophy* (trans. G. Adey and D. Frisby), London and Boston, Routledge, 1980, p. 162.

[37] Ibid., p. 163.

[38] Ibid., p. 164.

[39] Ibid., p. 168.

[40] Ibid.

[41] Ibid., p. 169.

[42] Ibid.
[43] Ibid., p. 170.
[44] Ibid.
[45] Ibid., p. 172.
[46] Ibid., p. 185.
[47] Ibid., p. 186.
[48] Quoted in T. McCarthy, *The Critical Theory of Jürgen Habermas,* Cambridge, Mass. MIT Press; Cambridge, Polity, 1984, p. 183.
[49] Ibid., pp. 183–184.
[50] Ibid., p. 262.
[51] T. A. McCarthy, 'A Theory of Communicative Competence', *Philosophy of the Social Sciences,* 3, 1973, p. 154.
[52] See J. Habermas, *Theory and Practice* (trans. J. Viertel), London, Heinemann, 1974, esp. pp. 1–40.
[53] See, especially, M. Horkheimer, *Critical Theory* (trans. M. J. O'Connell *et al.*), New York, St. Louis, San Francisco and Toronto, Herder & Herder, 1972.
[54] This was one of the issues in the so-called 'Positivist Dispute' and in Habermas's later confrontation with Luhmann. See, T. W. Adorno *et al., The Positivist Dispute in German Sociology* (trans. G. Adey and D. Frisby). London, Heinemann; New York, Harper & Row, 1976; Jürgen Habermas and Niklas Luhmann, *Theorie de Gesellschaft oder Sozialtechnologie — Was leistet die Systemforschung?,* Frankfurt, Suhrkamp, 1971.
[55] See J. Habermas, *Theorie des kommunikativen Handelns,* 2 vols., Frankfurt, Suhrkamp, 1981. The first volume has appeared in translation as *A Theory of Communicative Action* (trans. T. McCarthy), Cambridge, Mass, MIT Press, 1985.

5

Society as Second Nature

5.1 SOCIETY AS A SET OF SOCIAL RELATIONS

The concept of society found in Marx (1818–1883), the last social theorist whom we will consider, may usefully be seen as rooted in a double critique, which if accepted has implications for most of the conceptions discussed so far in this book. Marx simultaneously attacks two 'abstractions' which he thinks bedevil social theorizing: first, the abstraction of the individual; second, the abstraction of society itself. He rejects any conception of the individual as an isolated monad, who can be considered independently of historical and social context. For him — much as for Montesquieu — individuals are always and everywhere first of all *social* individuals. But he is equally concerned to repudiate, as a reification, any notion of society as a 'subject', existing over and apart from interacting individuals. These two abstractions, for Marx, are integrally related to one another.

They are also, in his view, more than just conceptual or ideational errors. For Marx, theorizing about society in particular ways itself has historical and social preconditions. He held a materialist theory of consciousness: ideas are not free-floating, but 'the independent expression in thought of the existing world' [1]. He accordingly ascribes a definite historical origin to these twin sociological illusions, as he sees them. They reflect, he thinks, the social relations of *bürgerliche Gesellschaft* — civil, or bourgeois society — itself. They articulate these, however, in distorted, ideological ways. The roots of these erroneous conceptions lie in the immediate forms in which we experience bourgeois social relations — their phenomenal forms, as Marx called them — which he held to be systematically misleading.

The critique of the 'abstract individual' is a remarkably consistent theme in Marx's writing over forty years. In what is the first (and remains the most wide-ranging) systematic statement of the historical materialist viewpoint, *The German Ideology* (with Engels, 1845–46), Marx repeatedly ridicules the Young Hegelian philosophers of his time for the 'speculative constructions' [2] which underpin their ideologies. Prominent among these are their notions of the human individual. Stirner's conception of the individual is the 'individual of the philosophical conception, the individual separate from his actuality and existing only in thought, "Man" as such' [3]. Feuerbach, likewise, 'says "Man" instead of "real historical man" ': whereas 'the abstract individual whom he analyses belongs in reality to a particular form of society' [4]. Semmig 'abandons the real behaviour of the individual and again takes refuge in this indescribable, inaccessible, peculiar nature' [5]. For Marx, however, 'the nature which develops in human history — the genesis of human society — is man's *real* nature' [6]. Grün's notion of Man is similarly 'a complete chimera. Man must be viewed in his real historical activity and existence' [7]. Writing on the German economist Adolph Wagner, nearly forty years later, Marx's criticism is the same:

> 'Man'? If this means the category 'Man', then in general he has 'no' needs; if the man who confronts nature in isolation, then he has to be conceived as a non-gregarious animal; if a man already present in some form of society — and this Herr Wagner presupposes, for his 'Man' possesses, if not a university education then at any rate language — then the determinate character of this social man should have been set out at the beginning, i.e., the determinate character of the community [*Gemeinwesen*] in which he lives [8].

Marx extends these points in his General Introduction (1857) to the *Grundrisse* (1857–58) [9]. Considering the proper analytic starting-point for a political economy, he argues that 'individuals producing in society — hence socially determined individual production — is of course the point of departure'. He then attacks 'the unimaginative conceits of the eighteenth-century Robinsonades', the 'individual and isolated' hunters and fishermen on whom Smith and Ricardo premise their economics. The same error, he thinks, underpins Rousseau's *contrat social,* 'which brings naturally independent, autonomous subjects into relation and connection by contract'. In fact, Marx argues, this isolated individual subject is the specifically *modern* individual — 'the product on one side of the dissolution of the feudal forms of society, on the other side of the new forces of production developed since the sixteenth century' — 'whose existence they project into the past'.

Marx's argument here strikingly anticipates Durkheim's in *The Division of Labour in Society:*

Only in the eighteenth century, in 'civil society', do the various forms of social connectedness confront the individual as a mere means towards his private purposes, as external necessity. But the epoch which produces this standpoint, that of the isolated individual, is also that of the hitherto most developed social (from this standpoint, general) relations. The human being is in the most literal sense a *zoon politikon* [social animal], not merely a gregarious animal, but an animal which can individuate itself only in the midst of society. Production by an isolated individual outside society [. . .] is as much of an absurdity as is the development of language without individuals living *together* and talking to each other. [10]

For Marx, in short, individuals are irreducibly social and cannot adequately be described independently of their social context. This also means — a thesis we will return to — that they must be grasped *historically,* for that social context, and in consequence the nature of individuals, changes through time. Indeed for Marx 'all history is nothing but a continuous transformation of human nature', 'the creation of man through human labour' [11].

But if he thus stresses the inherent sociality of individuals, Marx is equally concerned to avoid reifying society. He attacks Stirner for treating 'society as a person, a subject' [12] (contrast Durkheim: 'indeed a society is a being, a person'). Matthäi is castigated for conceiving society 'not as the interaction of the constituent "individual lives", but as a separate existence which undergoes another and separate interaction with these "individual lives" ' [13]. Criticizing Bauer, Marx derides any view of ' "society as the subject" ' as 'speculative-idealistic, i.e. fantastic', a mystification whereby 'the consecutive series of interrelated individuals connected with each other can be conceived as a single individual, which accomplishes the mystery of generating itself' [14].

'What is society whatever its form?', Marx asks in a famous letter of 1846, and answers: 'the product of human reciprocal action' [15]. This concurs with his conclusion, in the Paris manuscripts of two years before, that 'above all we must avoid postulating "society" again as an abstraction *vis-à-vis* the individual. The individual *is the social being*' [16]. Marx goes on to make a point we mooted earlier against Durkheim's dualism of individual and social:

his [the individual's] manifestations of life — even if they may not appear in the direct form of *communal* manifestations carried out in association with others — *are* therefore an expression and confirmation of *social life*. Man's individual and species-life are not *different*. [17].

Unlike for Weber, but with Winch, solitary prayer would for Marx be a social action. For as he summarizes it: 'my *own* existence *is* social activity' [18].

Like the 'abstract' individual, for Marx the reified conception of society also has a basis in material experience. In brief:

In history up to the present it is certainly an empirical fact that separate individuals have, with the broadening of their activity into world-historical activity, become more and more enslaved under a power alien to them [. . .] a power which has become more and more enormous and, in the last instance, turns out to be the *world market*. [19]

In bourgeois society, 'the product of human reciprocal action' is indeed *experienced* as an alien force, external to individuals, Adam Smith's 'hidden hand'. In Marx's view, this estrangement is the material foundation for reified concepts of society. *The German Ideology* roots this alienation in the division of labour:

Within the division of labour [social] relationships are bound to acquire independent existence in relation to individuals. All relations can be expressed in language only in the form of concepts. That these general ideas and concepts are looked upon as mysterious forces is the necessary result of the fact that the real relations, or which they are the expression, have acquired independent existence. [20].

Marx's analysis was to deepen after 1846 — it becomes clear that he is talking of particular social forms of division of labour, which reach their apotheosis in bourgeois society — but he makes essentially the same point some twenty years later in the first volume of *Capital* (1867). 'The same division of labour that turns [people] into independent private producers, also frees the social process of production and the relations of the individual producers to each other within that process, from all dependence on the will of those producers' [21]. In this 'form of society [. . .] the behaviour of men in the social process of production is purely atomic. Hence their relations to each other [. . .] assume a material character independent of their control and conscious individual action' [22]. What results is 'a whole network of social relations spontaneous in their growth and entirely beyond the control of the actors' [23].

This 'independence' of society *vis-à-vis* individuals is real, not imaginary. In that sense Marx would allow *bourgeois* society many Durkheimian attributes. Where he differs from Durkheim is that rather than seeing the externality of society as a permanent and necessary feature of human sociation as such, he regards its conditions as historically specific. In the Hegelian terminology Marx favoured in his youth, objectification — the expression of human capacities in the objective world humans produce — is universal, but alienation — the escaping of this social world from human control, with a consequent inability of people to recognize themselves and their own authorship in it — is not.

Reified conceptions of society thus for Marx specifically reflect the real alienation of social relations from their participants characteristic of bourgeois society. Had he been living at the end of the century, Marx would have been likely to argue that Durkheim's sui generis postulate merely generalizes — illicitly — from the estranged or 'alien' forms in which specifically bourgeois social relations present themselves in the experience of their participants. He might also have argued, conversely, that methodological individualist sociologies like Max Weber's equally generalize from, and are equally vitiated by, the appearance of individual independence characteristic of 'civil society' — an appearance he sees as ultimately illusory, given the reality of social connectedness through division of labour. Both polarities of the standard sociological debate, he might suggest, rest on an uncritical inscription within social theorizing of contemporary forms of appearance, the raw data of bourgeois social experience.

What, then, is Marx's own viewpoint on society? Once again, he is remarkably consistent in his pronouncements over the years. In his famous 'Theses on Feuerbach' (1845) he insists that 'the human essence is no abstraction inherent in each single individual. In its reality it is the ensemble of the social relations' [24]. He had written to Feuerbach himself the previous year making a similar point: 'The unity of man with man, which is based on the real differences between men, the concept of the human species brought down from the heaven of abstraction to the real earth, what is this but the concept of *society!*' [25]. Polemicizing against Proudhon, fifteen years later in the *Grundrisse,* he elaborates on what he means by the latter:

so-called contemplation from the standpoint of society means nothing more than the overlooking of the *differences* which express the *social relation* (relation of bourgeois society). Society does not consist of individuals, but expresses the sum of interrelations, the relations within which these individuals stand. As if someone were to say: Seen from the perspective of society, there are no slaves and no citizens: both are human beings. Rather, they are that outside society. To be a slave, to be a citizen, are social characteristics, relations between human beings A and B. Human being A, as such, is not a slave. He is a slave in and through society. [26]

Society is not, then, a self-acting subject sui generis: 'its only subjects are the individuals, but individuals in mutual relationships, which they produce and reproduce anew' [27]. But nor is society reducible to these individual subjects as such, considered independently of these relations. That would be to consider individuals abstractly and ahistorically. Society is, rather, the *set of relationships* that links individuals. Individuals — and, as we will see, objects — acquire social characteristics in virtue of their positions within these relations.

Central to this conception of society is an important point that emerges from both of the last two quotations we have given. Because is relational, it is integrally a system of *differences,* and those characteristics which mark individuals as social are therefore ones which also *differentiate* them as individuals in definite ways: for instance as master or servant, husband or wife. This means that society is not homogeneous. It is rather, in Marx's own concept, a *contradictory* unity. Where, as in most societies Marx analyses, the contradictions within social relations are antagonistic, society emerges as an entity to which possibilities of conflict, movement and change are inbuilt. It is thus, from the start, implicitly a *dynamic* whole.

5.2   SOCIETY AS MATERIAL INTERCOURSE

People are related to one another in society in a multitude of ways. But for Marx certain kinds of social relation are fundamental, and these provide the basis for distinguishing different forms of society, or as he called them 'socio-economic formations':

Since we are dealing with the Germans, who are devoid of premises, we must begin by stating the first premise of all human existence, and, therefore, of all history, the premise, namely, that men must be in a position to live in order to "make history". But life involves before everything else eating and drinking, a habitation, clothing and many other things. The first historical act is thus the production of the means to satisfy these needs, the production of material life itself. And indeed this is an historical act, a fundamental condition of all history, which today, as thousands of years ago, must daily and hourly be fulfilled merely in order to sustain human life. [28].

For Marx the most basic of social relations are relations of production — those social relations established within 'the production of material life itself' — and an adequate sociology must accordingly be a materialistic one. Unlike for Simmel or Winch, there is a privileged starting-point for sociological analysis. It lies in human needs (and their historic development).

We must ask, then, what Marx understands by social relations of production. This is a trickier (and a more contentious) issue than it might at first sight appear. All production, he says in *The German Ideology,* involves two kinds of relation:

the production of life, both of one's own in labour and of fresh life in procreation [. . .] appears as a double relationship: on the one hand as a natural, on the other as a social relationship. By social we understand the co-operation of several individuals, no matter under what conditions, in what manner and to what end. [29].

Production always involves, first, relations between people and nature. The concept Marx uses to analyse this is that of the *labour process,* wherein people labour, with the aid of instruments of production of one sort or another, to transform natural raw materials into products which meet their needs [30]. This process is 'the everlasting nature-imposed condition of human existence' and is thus 'independent of every social phase of that existence, or, rather [. . .] common to every such phase' [31]. But, second, production equally involves relations between people themselves. 'All production is appropriation of nature on the part of an individual *within and through a definite form of society*' [32]. This sociological emphasis is central to Marx's understanding of production, as he makes very clear:

In the process of production, human beings do not only enter into a relation with Nature. They produce only by working together in a specific manner and by reciprocally exchanging their activities. In order to produce, they enter into definite connections and relations with one another, and only within these social connections and relations does their connection with Nature, i.e. production, take place. [33].

In *Capital* Marx refers to both these kinds of relation — relations 'between man and man, and between man and Nature' — as 'the social relations within the sphere of material life' [34]. There is an important issue buried in this, since it is not immediately evident why Marx should refer to the people/nature relation as a social relation. But for him, material objects as well as people enter into the set of relations which make up society, and themselves acquire social characteristics in consequence. Objects — for instance the goods people exchange — may mediate relations between people, and real or attributed qualities of those objects come to express those relations. Thus, for example, for Marx the value of commodities is a mode of expressing the labour-time socially necessary to their production, and commodity price movements the means through which labour-inputs are equilibriated between different branches of production. In the same way the class relation between bourgeoisie and the working class — in which, for Marx, the former appropriates the unpaid surplus labour of the latter — is manifested in the capacity of capital to generate profit or bear interest. This aspect of Marx's concept is basic to his theory of fetishism, which we will discuss below.

The key point here, however, is that for Marx production — the fundamental material condition of all social life — is *intrinsically* a social activity. And this has, for him, an important implication for how we conceive society itself:

it is quite obvious from the start that there exists a materialistic connection of men with one another, which is determined by their needs and their mode of production, and which is as old as men themselves. This connection is ever taking on new forms, and thus presents a 'history' independently of the existence of any political or religious nonsense which would especially hold men together. [35]

Minimally, any society, whatever else it may comprise, involves this 'materialistic connection' — a set of social relations of production — and this is the distinctive starting-point of Marx's sociology. But at times, he goes so far as virtually to equate society as such with these relations. Thus in the *Grundrisse,* for instance, he writes that 'when we consider bourgeois society in the long view and as a whole, then the final result of the process of social production always appears as the society itself, i.e. the human being itself in its social relations' [36]. In *The German Ideology* he repeatedly denies that politics, law, religion, art, and so on, have any history independent of this 'materialistic connection' [37]. This may appear an extremely reductionist viewpoint. We shall argue it is not, if Marx is properly interpreted.

Marx's most famous — or infamous — summary of his views on the connection between production relations and social life as a whole is to be found in his Preface to *The Critique of Political Economy* (1859):

> The totality of these relations of production constitutes the economic structure of society, the real foundation, on which arises a legal and political superstructure and to which correspond definite forms of social consciousness. The mode of production of material life conditions the general process of social, political and intellectual life. [38]

This claim — a substantive one, which in no way simply follows from an acknowledgement that material production is a universal precondition of human society (any more than it follows that because language is equally a precondition, social structures are determined by the laws of grammar) — is perhaps *the* most distinctive hallmark of Marx's approach. Where for Durkheim society is a moral entity, or for Winch an interpretive community, for Marx it is first and foremost a set of material relations, the nexus of production relations whose totality comprises its 'economic structure'. The problem, however, is how exactly this claim is to be interpreted. There are few more contentious issues in Marxist theory [39].

The standard reading of this and related passages in Marx extracts two fundamental postulates. These are first, that any society can be divided into an 'economic' base and a legal, political and ideological 'superstructure'; second, that the former 'determines' the latter. The base comprises relations of production. In conventional Marxist accounts, these are normally held to be relations directly entailed in the labour process (for instance, forms of cooperation and division of labour 'in the workshop') and relations of control over its elements (labour, raw materials, instruments of production, products). In other words, a universal and substantive definition of production relations is offered in advance, at the level of general theory. Production relations are usually expressed as property relations, though strictly speaking they are not identical with them (legal forms belonging in the superstructure), and are the foundation of social classes — for Marx the heart, in most societies, of social structure.

The superstructure is, in most orthodox accounts, everything else in society: specifically it includes law, politics and ideology. The 'determination' of the superstructure by the base is normally (though not invariably) understood in straightforward causal terms. Most accounts, however, allow superstructures some 'relative autonomy' and see this determination only as 'ultimate', and modern Marxism has thrown up a variety of more or less sophisticated models of 'structural causality' to conceptualize this relation. In our view this entire enterprise is misconceived, both as a conception of society and an expression of Marx's own thinking.

Leaving aside general arguments about the base/superstructure model as such [40], it is notable that Marx does not, in the 1859 Preface, anywhere say what kind of social relation can or cannot be a relation of production. He simply says that the totality of such relations makes up the 'economic structure' of society. In other words, he defines this 'economic structure' by (undefined) production relations rather than production relations by their 'economic' character as conventionally understood. The same is true of property relations, which for the Preface 'merely express the same thing [production relations] in legal terms': as he writes elsewhere, 'to define bourgeois property is nothing else than to give an exposition of all the social relations of bourgeois production' [41]. What then *is* a production relation, this fundamental category in terms of which both economic structure and property are themselves defined? In fact, Marx treats the category of production relations as an extremely open-ended one. We believe this is an essential feature of the concept, and not a sign of analytic sloppiness on Marx's part.

In *Grundrisse,* he offers this definition: 'human life has since time immemorial rested on production and, in one way or another, on *social* production, whose relations we call, precisely, economic relations' [42]. Elsewhere he speaks simply of 'the social relations within which individuals produce' [43]. We know of no text in Marx which provides warrant for the restricted category of production relations employed by orthodox perspectives. On the other hand, there are substantive analyses in his work with which the latter are simply not compatible [44]. In the case of feudal society, for instance, Marx argues in *Capital* that surplus extraction from peasants by lords could not take place without 'other than economic pressure': 'conditions of personal dependence are requisite, a lack of personal freedom [. . .] and being tied to the soil as its accessory, bondage in the true sense of the word' [45]. The 'direct relationship of lordship and servitude' [46] — in other words a political relation — is thus a 'social relation within which individuals produce', and without which they could not begin to produce in that way. Hence, 'personal dependence here characterizes the social relations of production just as much as it does the other spheres of life organized on the basis of that production [. . .] personal dependence forms the groundwork of society' [47]. In *Grundrisse* he similarly argues that in primitive communal modes of production, 'communality of blood, language, customs' is 'the first presupposition' for 'real appropriation through the labour process' (and adds 'property therefore means belonging to a clan') [48]. Here it is kinship relations which are integral to 'the social relations within which individuals produce' — a finding corroborated by much modern Marxist anthropology. The centrality of 'extra-economic coercion' to feudal exploitation is likewise confirmed by much modern Marxist work in medieval history [49]. Either analysis makes nonsense of the standard base/superstructure model. In both cases, 'superstructural' relations emerge as *internal* to the 'economic structure' of society itself. If so, they can hardly be determined by this economic structure in any normal causal sense since it evidently presupposes them.

Marx himself stipulates in *The German Ideology* that:

definite individuals who are productively active in a definite way enter into these definite social and political relations. Empirical observation must in each separate intance bring out empirically, and without any mystification and speculation, the connection of the social and political structure with production [50].

Had Marxists taken this seriously, they could have generated neither a universal model of society of the base/superstructure kind nor the sort of restricted category of production relations it sustains. For on this methodology 'the connection of the social and political structure with production' — what, in any given case, production relations *are* — could not properly be the object of a general theory, whether posited *a priori* or arrived at inductively. What is, or is not, a relation of production could only be ascertained through empirical inquiry in each specific case. The only general concept of production relations consistent with this is precisely the one Marx offers — an empirically open-ended one. Production relations are, simply, all those social relations presupposed to a way in which people produce. What in any specific instance these relations will be is an ineluctably empirical question.

In passing, we would make two further comments. First, the entire base/superstructure conception is built on a metaphor which Marx uses surprisingly infrequently, and then inconsistently: at times he can be read as referring to institutions, but as often (and in greater accord with his general viewpoint) he uses the term 'superstructure' to designate *ideological forms* — philosophical, juridical, political, artistic — in which people become conscious of (and frequently mistake) their social relations [51]. On this reading the base/superstructure metaphor becomes an uncontentious restatement of Marx's materialist theory of consciousness rather than a putative model of society. Alasdair MacIntyre long ago developed this argument:

> As Marx depicts it the relation between basis and superstructure is fundamentally not only not mechanical, it is not even causal. What may be misleading is Marx's Hegelian vocabulary. Marx certainly talks of the basis 'determining' the superstructure and of a 'correspondence' between them. But the reader of Hegel's *Logic* will realise that what Marx envisages is something to be understood in terms of the way in which the nature of the concept of a given class, for example may determine the concept of membership of that class [. . .] The economic basis of a society is not its tools, but the people co-operating using these particular tools in the manner necessary to their use, and the superstructure consists of the social consciousness moulded by and the shape of this co-operation. [52].

It is in this spirit that we should interpret such remarks of Marx's as 'every *social* form of property has morals of its own', or 'political economy expresses moral laws in its own way' [53] — less as reductionist statements than as indicators of the capaciousness of his concepts of property/production relations themselves, particular forms of morality (or politics, or law) being internal to these relations rather than, as on the standard model, their epiphenomena.

Second, it is tempting to argue that the translation of the metaphor into such a model has similar roots to the reification of society discussed above. It is precisely in *bourgeois* society that 'the economy' first appears as an independent sphere, separable from other social relations, and polity and law also assume clearly separable institutional forms [54]. Conversely the limitations of the base/superstructure model become most glaringly evident so soon as we try and apply it to pre-capitalist modes of production. Like the reified concept of society and the abstracted individual Marx himself criticizes, the orthodox model derives its plausibility from its correspondence to the phenomenal forms of bourgeois society, but its inadequacy becomes apparent so soon as we move beyond those boundaries—whether to other societies, or beneath the surface of 'civil society' itself.

For Marx, then, people's 'materialistic connection' — their production relations — is the groundwork of society, and different types or historical epochs of society are distinguished by the particular forms this connection takes. The *mode of production,* or 'way in which people produce their means of subsistence', is therefore his fundamental unit of sociological analysis and historical periodization. The main such modes of production — and forms of society — Marx distinguishes are the primitive communal, Asiatic, ancient, feudal and capitalist [55]. He denies that social life as a whole can be understood independently of this materialistic connection, and indeed goes further than this to argue that production relations are the core relations of social life.

The relations, specifically, through which the social surplus over subsistence is extracted—class relations, in most forms of society—are for Marx the fundamental components of social structure, and the major empirical focus of his sociology:

> The specific economic form, in which unpaid surplus labour is pumped out of direct producers, determines the relationship of rulers and ruled, as it grows directly out of production itself, and, in turn, reacts upon it as a determining element. Upon this, however, is founded the entire formation of the economic community which grows up out of the production relations themselves, thereby simultaneously its specific political form. It is always the direct relationship of the owners of the conditions of production to the direct producers [. . .] which reveals the innermost secret, the hidden basis of the entire social structure, and with it the political form of the relation of sovereignty and dependence, in short, the corresponding specific form of the state. This does not prevent the same economic basis [. . .] from showing infinite variations and gradations in appearance, which can be ascertained only by analysis of the empirically given circumstances. [56]

On condition that we understand production relations in the broad way we have outlined, this need not be interpreted as a reductionist claim or imply an unduly economistic sociology or historiography. The passage we have just quoted, for instance, occurs in the midst of (and can only be understood when related to) the eminently non-reductionist discussion of feudal relations cited above. We might still jib at any implied claim that *all* aspects of social life can be explained from this foundation, and prefer to treat it as a starting-point of analysis only: this would be the present authors' preference. To do so would be in accord with Marx's empirical injunctions, if at odds with some of his grander pronouncements.

In this context, however, one major criticism of Marx does need to be made. In a passage we quoted previously from *The German Ideology*, Marx includes within 'the production of material life' not only production of material objects, but also production 'of fresh life in procreation'. 'The third circumstance which, from the very outset, enters into historical development, is that men, who daily remake their own life, begin to make other men, to propagate their own kind: the relation between man and woman, parents and children, the *family*' [57]. In the same text he sees 'the nucleus, the first form' of both division of labour and property as lying in 'the family, where wife and children are the slaves of the husband' [58]. It has to be said that these fragmentary suggestions were not, in general, taken further by Marx. They remain gestural. His conceptual framework — in common with virtually all classical sociologies — is one which systematically marginalizes issues of biological reproduction of the human species, and its social organization through gender and familial relations.

One can argue that there is an inconsistency in Marx himself here — testimony to a 'capturing', perhaps, of his own analytic framework by dominant 'self-understood forms of social life' [59] akin to the ideological distortions he himself analysed in others? Notwithstanding these piecemeal observations in *The German Ideology*, Marx's concept of production effectively reduces to that of production of material goods alone: the world reflected here and expressed as theory is the bourgeois one where 'home' and 'work' are separated and only the latter registers as 'productive'. Yet in reality, production of *people* is as fundamental to the possibility of social existence as production of their means of subsistence. They have to be produced, moreover, as *social* individuals. This is as intrinsically a part of people's 'materialistic connection' as their 'mode of production' as Marx conceived it. Marx recognized this in general terms, but this recognition did not extend to how he actually analysed modes and relations of production. For production of people entails family forms, nurturing of children, and much else, and these do not normally figure in either his general conceptual lexicon or as major elements in his substantive analyses of capitalism or any other form of society. And where Marxists, from Engels onwards, have looked at gender relations at all the tendency has been to try and explain them as epiphenomena of modes of production as traditionally construed.

We would argue, however, that the implication of recognizing that biological and social reproduction of individuals is as essential to people's 'materialistic connection' as production of goods, is that both Marxist analytic categories, and Marxist substantive analyses need comprehensively to be rethought. If 'production' centrally includes production of people themselves, then amongst its key social relations must be gender relations. This implies, amongst other things, that patriarchy is as definitive an aspect of present social relations as capitalism, and gender as essential an axis of social structure as class. Thinking these issues through cannot simply be a matter of 'adding on' to extant Marxist analyses presumed to be adequate; the questions go deeper. Similar points could be made about ethnicity, or locality, or any other social differences through which the way in which people 'renew themselves, even as they renew the world of wealth they create' is empirically organized [60].

In short, while people's 'materialistic connection' may as Marx contents be an adequate starting-point for sociological analysis, the concept of mode of production, as conventionally understood, is not. It excludes too much of what does materially relate people. Similarly, relations of *reproduction* (of people, not goods) need to be given as much weight in any genuinely materialist sociology as relations of production. If a single Marxist category is to be of any use for bringing within a unified conceptual framework the considerable variety of kinds of social relation (and social difference) through which 'the final result of the process of social production always appears as the society itself, i.e. the human being itself in its social relations' [61], it is, we suggest, likely to be that of social division of labour. Marx pointed out this road in *The German Ideology*. He did not go down it.

5.3 SOCIETY AS HISTORICAL PROCESS

We have seen then that for Marx society is a set of social relations — it is thus a contradictory unity, an ensemble of individual differences — and that primary among these relations are those which comprise people's 'materialistic connection'. A third, and equally crucial dimension of Marx's concept of society is a *historical* one, and for him, at least, this is implied in the first two. Production is crucial to the concept of society not simply as a presupposition of human existence, but equally because of the kind of activity it is. In production, Marx argues, people actively transform both their material environment and themselves, and it is this capacity which specifically differentiates humanity as a species and makes history both a possible and a necessary aspect of their social existence. 'The first *historical* act of these individuals distinguishing them from animals is not that they think, but that they begin to *produce their means of subsistence*' [62]. 'Men have history because they must *produce* their life' [63].

The point need hardly be laboured. But in this context — and as an interesting parallel with the dual critique of abstract individual/reified society discussed above — it is worth noting that Marx similarly attacked both idealist *and* materialist historiographies of his day. The former, predictably enough, he castigated for excluding people's 'materialistic connection' from historical inquiry [64]. But he equally condemned 'so-called *objective* historiography' for 'treating the historical conditions independent of activity' [65]. This is the constant refrain of the 'Theses on Feuerbach'. The first thesis sees 'the chief defect of all hitherto existing materialism' as 'that the thing, reality, sensuousness, is conceived only in the form of the object or of *contemplation,* but not as *sensuous human activity, practice,* not subjectively' [66]. The 'active side' was developed — albeit abstractly — by idealism. The implication for concepts of society is spelled out in the third thesis:

> The materialist doctrine that men are products of circumstances and upbringing, and that, therefore, changed men are products of other circumstances and changed upbringing, forgets that it is men who change circumstances and that is essential to educate the educator himself. Hence, this doctrine necessarily arrives at dividing society into two parts, one of which is superior to society [. . .]
> The coincidence of the changing of circumstances and of human activity can be conceived and rationally understood only as revolutionising practice. [67]

Any materialist doctrine which sees individuals solely as passive pro-ducts of a social environment external and prior to them will have difficulty in accounting for how that environment itself changes. Logically we might evade the problem, but only at the cost of a reification unacceptable to Marx — what he refers to here as the dividing of society into two parts, one of which is superior to society. For Marx, the way out of the dilemma is to recognize that social relations, and particularly those of material life, are not simply an external environment. They are forms of (social) individuals' *own* activity, their 'revolutionizing practice'. 'Just as society itself produces *man as man,* so is society *produced* by him' [68]. In consideriang society we are dealing, as Marx always insists we are, with people's activities.

Because those activities are material and always take place in a preconstructed social context people are not 'free' to act as they wish: they enter into relations which are 'independent of their will' [69]. The abstract individual is no basis for an analysis of social action. But equally, because those activities are transformative, society is inherently a changing, dynamic entity — it has a history. A more prosaic, but no less relevant statement of the same point is found in Marx's oft-quoted remark from the *Eighteenth Brumaire* (1852) that 'men make their own history, but not of their own free will; not under circumstances they themselves have chosen but under the given and inherited circumstances with which they are directly confronted' [70]. Both of Marx's emphases — that people are the sole history makers, but never *ex nihilo* — matter equally.

Marx's substantive theory of historical development and social change must be understood within this general perspective. Once again he summarizes his view in the 1859 Preface:

> At a certain stage of their development, the material productive forces of society come into conflict with the existing relations of production or — this merely expresses the same thing in legal terms — with the property relations within the framework of which they have operated hitherto. From forms of development of the productive forces these relations turn into their fetters. Then begins an era of social revolution. [71].

In *The German Ideology,* Marx bluntly states that 'all collisions in history have their origin, according to our view, in the contradiction between the productive forces and the form of intercourse' [*Verkehrsform*; later Marx used the concept of relations of production — *Produktionsverhältnisse* — to express the same idea] [72]. It is, in short, conflict between forces and relations of production which impels historical development, and in particular explains transition from one form of society (ancient, feudal, capitalist, etc.) to another. But once more, exactly what is meant by this is contentious [73].

The crudest interpretation is a technological determinism, and there are as usual passages in Marx which, when taken in isolation, support this view [74]. But this supposes that when Marx speaks of developing productive forces he is referring to technology alone. There are, however, numerous occasions where Marx uses the concept much more widely to embrace any and all forces through which human productive capacities are developed. Thus, for instance, he concludes from a passage we have already quoted on production as a 'double relationship', both natural and social, that 'a certain mode of production, or industrial stage, is always combined with a certain mode of co-operation, or social stage, and this mode of co-operation is itself a "productive force" ' [75]. He sees a 'communal economy' (socialism) as 'in itself [. . .] a new productive force' [76]. Elsewhere in the same text he counterposes 'industrial productive forces' and 'productive forces [. . .] based for the most part on association and the community' [77], and treats both money and the working class itself as productive forces [78]. In *Capital* he discusses science, and above all forms of socialized labour, as productive forces in their own right [79].

Indeed, consonant with the wider analysis of alienation touched on above, *The German Ideology* offers a critique of the reduction of what are for Marx always *social* productive forces to the material objects in which they are embodied:

> The social power, i.e., the multiplied productive force, which arises through the co-operation of different individuals as it is determined by the division of labour, appears to these individuals, since their co-operation is not voluntary but has come about naturally, not as their own united power, but as an alien force existing outside them, of the origin and goal of which they are ignorant, which they thus cannot control, which on the contrary passes through a peculiar series of phases and stages independent of the will and the action of man, nay even being the prime governor of these. [80].

With the development of division of labour 'the productive forces appear as a world for themselves' and 'have, as it were, taken on material form and are for the individuals no longer the forces of the individuals' [81]. But in reality, for Marx, 'the history of the evolving productive forces' is nothing but 'the history of the development of the forces of the individuals themselves' [82]. In *Grundrisse* he speaks of 'forces of production and social relations' as but 'two different sides of the development of the social individual' [83].

Arguably, then, to equate productive forces with technology alone is to reify them. If the broader interpretation proposed here is accepted, then Marx's contradiction between evolving productive forces and moribund production relations becomes a contradiction internal to society — the ensemble of social relations — rather than between technology and society. It may advantageously be seen as a contradiction between the *capacities* created by people in their social production and the particular social *forms* in which these are temporarily incarnated. Specifically, for Marx, new productive forces are embodied in new social classes and it is their struggles which push history forward.

The key point for our purposes, however, is that for Marx society's basis in people's materialistic connection — their productive activities — implies not only a generalized dynamism as nature is transformed, but specific *social* antagonisms as new forces are developed, linked with new social classes, which undermine previous social relationships. This contradiction — and the systematic conflicts it implies — are for Marx essential features of society. Difference, conflict, and the change that results, are not in Marx's view deviant but thoroughly normal and expected societal characteristics, at least so long as classes exist.

5.4 SOCIETY AS A MIRAGE

One final theme implicit in much of the foregoing needs to be further developed [84]. For Marx society is nothing but the mutual interrelations of individuals, and its structure, in the final analysis, no more than the regularities in their patterns of interaction through time. Society is historical process, as E. P. Thompson understands the term [85]. At the same time it does not always *appear* as such to its participants. On the contrary, social relations frequently appear — and are accordingly grasped by social theories — as if they were both timeless and authorless. In his early writings of the 1840s Marx analyses this phenomenon — one most developed in bourgeois society — as alienation, in *Capital* as 'fetishism'. In fetishism there is a twofold inversion: it 'metamorphoses the social, economic character impressed on things in the process of social production into a natural character stemming from the material nature of these things' [86]; and it correspondingly represents the historical as universal. The basis of this illusion is material: it lies in the forms in which society presents itself in the experience of its participants.

For Marx, the phenomenal forms in which society's essential relations manifest themselves to individuals may mislead, and these essential relations may not be transparent to actors. Importantly for his concept of society, this is not, for Marx, a matter of people's errors of perception. It could not be, given his materialist theory of consciousness, for to see the deception as arising from false *consciousness* would be to concede the independence of consciousness from material experience which that theory denies. Rather, Marx holds that experience may *itself* mislead, and where this occurs it is a function of the character of the relations at issue. It is not that we mistake reality. Reality is sometimes structured in such a way as to deceive us. Society is sometimes like a mirage. Thus, to take a famous example, the substance of the wage contract for Marx is an unequal exchange. The labourer is paid a value determined by the production costs of his means of subsistence, but once employed creates a value in excess of this which the capitalist pockets as profit. It appears, however, as if the wage is an equivalent for work done — the wage is ostensibly paid for the work, after its completion, by the piece or by the hour — and profit therefore appears to originate from capital not labour.

This has an important analytic implication. Marx, as we have seen, repeatedly insists on the empirical foundations of sociological analysis. But clearly, if phenomenal forms — the data of ordinary social experience — can systematically deceive, then an analysis which remains on the empirical level, 'the surface of society' as Marx called it, will simply reproduce that deception. This is exactly what Marx charges against the abstracted notions of the individual and reified concepts of society considered earlier. They simply replicate 'the illusion of the epoch'. Here, once again, we find in Marx — *mutatis mutandis* — sentiments strongly reminiscent of Durkheim:

> it is always necessary to distinguish between the material transfor-
> mation of the economic conditions of production, which can be
> determined with the precision of natural science, and the legal,
> political, religious, artistic, or philosophic — in short, ideological
> forms in which men become conscious of this conflict and fight it
> out. Just as one does not judge an individual by what he thinks
> about himself, so one cannot judge such a period of transforma-
> tion by its consciousness, but, on the contrary, this consciousness
> must be explained from the contradictions of material life. [87].

But, once again, Marx differs from Durkheim in that he does not consider this mystification an invariant of social life. He can envisage a form of society in which social relations are 'perfectly simple and intelligible', and 'the life-process of society' does 'strip off its mystical veil' [88]. Indeed, he regards pre-capitalist relations as a good deal more transparent to their participants than those of bourgeois society, and people's spontaneous consciousness in such societies as that much more accurate [89]. But in the absence of such conditions 'it is a work of science to resolve the visible, merely external movement into the true intrinsic movement' [90]. Scientific analysis therefore entails a *critique* of actors' common-sense conceptions of the social world and a demystification of the 'natural, self-understood forms of social life' [91] — the phenomenal forms — on which these conceptions are founded. That critique will both explain why people's common-sense consciousness takes the forms it does and show where and why it is erroneous.

Regrettably, there is no space here to elaborate in detail on Marx's critique as a form of analysis which goes 'behind' the phenomenal forms of everyday life and yet can nonetheless reasonably claim to be empirically grounded [92]. But Marx himself discusses his method in the 1857 General Introduction [93] — albeit at times confusedly — in terms of an analytic passage from the 'imagined concrete' to 'simple abstractions', then back again to a 'reproduction of the concrete by way of thought'. 'It seems to be correct', he says, 'to begin with the real and the concrete', for example in economics with the population. But the latter is 'an abstraction', unless analytically resolved into the classes of which it is made up, these into the elements on which they rest (wage-labour, capital), and these in turn into their presuppositions ('exchange, division of labour, prices, etc.'). Thus,

> if I were to begin with the population, this would be a chaotic conception of the whole, and I would then, by means of further determination, move analytically towards ever more simple concepts, from the imagined concrete towards ever thinner abstractions until I had arrived at the simplest determinations. From there the journey would have to be retraced until finally I had arrived at the population again, but this time not as the chaotic conception of a whole, but as a rich totality of many determinations and relations.

What Marx here calls 'concrete' and 'abstract' correspond to what we (following *Capital*) refer to respectively as phenomenal forms and essential relations.

This passage from 'concrete' to 'abstract' and back again may be exemplified by Marx's analysis of the capital-form. Capital appears, 'on the surface of society', simply as money which when productively invested is capable of increasing its value — of making a profit. This is, for Marx, a specifically fetishistic illusion, for the ability to command surplus-value (a social characteristic) appears to be inherent in the material forms of capital itself. But

> A negro is negro. He only becomes a slave in certain relations. A

cotton-spinning jenny is a machine for spinning cotton. It becomes *capital* only in certain relations. Torn from these relationships it is no more capital than gold in itself is *money* or sugar the price of sugar. [94]

For Marx, profit originates in the capital/labour exchange. Contrary to appearances, it is not capital itself which generates the additional value. The latter comes from the discrepancy between the value the labourer is paid in wages and the value he creates when productively employed.

The essential relation behind this is what Marx calls the 'double freedom of labour'. The process supposes, first, that workers are free to sell their labour-power to employers (unlike, for instance, slaves or serfs), and second, that they are 'free of' any means of production of their own through which they could' otherwise avoid the necessity to do so (unlike, for example, peasants or independent craftsmen). Means of production, in other words, must have become the private property of the employers. The essential relation expressed in the phenomenal form capital is thus, specifically, the class relation between a propertied bourgeoisie and a disposed working class. 'Severance of the conditions of production, on the one hand, from the producers, on the other [. . .] forms the *conception* of capital' [95]. Capital thus emerges, not as the (somewhat mysterious) thing it originally appeared to be, but as

a definite social production relation, belonging to a defiite historical formation of society, which is manifested in a thing and lends this thing a definite social character. [96]

This has an important corollary. Evidently 'this relation has no natural basis, neither is its social basis one that is common to all historical periods. It is clearly the result of a past historical development' [97]. Unearthing the essential relation which is phenomenally manifested in the capital-form in other words demonstrates the *historical* character — and specificity — of this form. Marx makes the point sharply against Political Economy:

The economists do not conceive capital as a relation. They *cannot* do so without at the same time conceiving it as a historically transitory, i.e., a relative, not an absolute, form of production. [98]

This bears on the second stage of analysis, the passage back from 'abstract (essential relations) to 'concrete' (phenomenal forms). For this, we believe, is essentially a matter of respecifying those as yet abstractly conceived essential relations precisely as the actions of real individuals over time, or historical process. In this way, Marx in *Capital,* in pages rich in historical detail, concretizes absolute surplus-value in terms of 'the struggle for the normal working day' and relative surplus-value as 'the strife of workmen and machine' [99]. Class relations take on substance in the same way in his *Eighteenth Brumaire.*

The critique of phenomenal forms, and historical specification of essential relations, are complementary and equally important moments of analysis. Marx comments on their relation in the *Grundrisse:*

our method indicates the points where historical investigation must enter in [. . .] In order to develop the laws of bourgeois economy [. . .] it is not necessary to write the real history of the relations of production. But the correct observation and deduction of these laws [. . .] always leads to primary equations [. . .] which point towards a past lying behind this system. These indications [. . .] then also offer the key to the understanding of the past — a work in its own right. [100]

The critique is not, of itself, a historical analysis. It yields what is still an abstract conception of social relations. Concepts like value, surplus-value, labour/capital relation are not in themselves adequate empirical descriptions of the activities of men and women in which, in the end, the essential relations to which they refer consist — and, for Marx, entirely consist. But critique is an essential prerequisite of historical analysis, because otherwise history would be blind — or more correctly, would remain trapped in 'the illusion of the epoch'. So long as capital, for instance, is apprehended simply as a thing, any search for its origins will focus on such issues as the abstemious habits of early capitalists (who, it is presumed, saved 'it') or the influx of precious metals — money's material embodiment — from America into early modern Europe. Only when we know that capital is a *relation* will we examine the factors Marx focuses on in *Capital* — spoliation of

Church property, enclosures, clearances, vagrancy law, and so on —
through which this relation was historically constituted [101].

But conversely, not to take this latter step — not to go beyond critique
to historical inquiry — is to remain with an abstract conception of social
relations, in which society is not yet apprehended as 'the real individuals,
their activity, and the material conditions under which they live' [102].
Arguably much recent Marxist theory, particularly of the 'structuralist'
variety, has made just this error of misplaced concreteness (or as Marx
himself called it, 'violent abstraction'). It has precipitately reified the
'abstract' categories of essential relations generated in Marx's critique,
treating these as real entities rather than conceptual means for the investigation of real entities.

That investigation, however, *is* a 'work in its own right', and an
empirically arduous one, for the empirical characteristics of real social
actors and events cannot be deduced from their general concepts. From this
point of view, a work like E. P. Thompson's *Making of the English
Working Class* is an epitome of Marxist sociology. And we may conclude
this discussion with some apt, and justly famous, remarks from that work
which admirably illustrate what we mean when we say that for Marx,
society must ultimately be grasped as historical process — neither more,
nor less, than 'the product of individuals' reciprocal action'. Thompson is
speaking of class, but the point applies equally to any other of the relations
which for Marx make up society:

> the notion of class entails the notion of historical relationship.
> Like any other relationship, it is a fluency which evades analysis if
> we attempt to stop it dead at any given moment and anatomize its
> structure. The finest-meshed sociological net cannot give us a
> pure specimen of class, any more than it can give us one of
> deference or of love. The relationship must always be embodied
> in real people and in a real context [. . .]
>
> There is today an ever-present tendency to suppose that class
> is a thing. This was not Marx's meaning, in his own historical
> writing, yet the error vitiates much latter-day 'Marxist' writing.
> 'It', the working class, is assumed to have a real existence, which
> can be defined almost mathematically — so many men who stand
> in a certain relation to the means of production [. . .]
>
> The question, of course, is how the individual got to be in this
> 'social role', and how the particular social organization (with its
> property-rights and structure of authority) got to be there. And
> these are historical questions. If we stop history at a given point,

then there are no classes but simply a multitude of individuals with a multitude of experiences. But if we watch these men over an adequate period of social change, we observe patterns in their relationships, their ideas, and their institutions. Class is defined by men as they live their own history, and, in the end, this its only definition [103].

REFERENCES

[1] K. Marx and F. Engels, *The German Ideology*, Moscow, Progress, 2nd printing, 1968, p. 102.

[2] See ibid., 64, 542; K. Marx and F. Engels, *The Holy Family*, in *Collected Works* (Moscow, London, New York, 1975 onwards; hereafter cited as *CW* plus volume number), vol. 4, pp. 57–61.

[3] *German Ideology*, p. 324.

[4] Ibid., p. 57; 'Theses on Feuerbach', ibid., p. 661.

[5] *German Ideology*, p. 524.

[6] K. Marx, Economic and philosophic manuscripts of 1844, *CW* 3, p. 303.

[7] *German Ideology*, pp. 576–577.

[8] Marginal notes on Wagner, *Lehrbuch der politischen Ökonomie. Theoretical Practice*, 5, 1972, pp. 45–46.

[9] General Introduction to K. Marx, *Grundrisse*, London, Penguin 1973. Quotations in this paragraph from pp. 83–84. Cf. Economic and philosophic mss, p. 271.

[10] General Introduction, p. 84. On language compare *German Ideology* pp. 42, 57; Notes on Wagner, pp. 45–46.

[11] K. Marx *The Poverty of Philosophy*, New York, International Publishers, 1973, p. 147; Economic and philosophic mss, p. 305.

[12] *German Ideology*, p. 224.

[13] Ibid., p. 536.

[14] Ibid., p. 50.

[15] Letter to Annenkov, 28 December 1846, with *Poverty of Philosophy*, p. 180.

[16] Economic and philosophic mss, p. 299.

[17] Ibid.

[18] Ibid., p. 298.

[19] *German Ideology*, p. 49.

[20] Ibid., p. 406.

[21] K. Marx, *Capital*, vol. 1, London, Lawrence & Wishart, 1970, p. 108.

[22] Ibid., pp. 92–93.

[23] Ibid., p. 112.

[24] 'Theses on Feuerbach', in *German Ideology,* p. 660.

[25] Letter to L. Feuerbach, 11 August 1844, *CW* 3, p. 354.

[26] *Grundrisse,* p. 265.

[27] Ibid., p. 712.

[28] *German Ideology,* p. 39.

[29] Ibid., p. 41.

[30] See *Capital,* vol. 1, ch. 7, sec. 1.

[31] Ibid., pp. 177, 184.

[32] General Introduction to *Grundrisse,* p. 87.

[33] *Wage Labour and Capital,* Moscow, Progress, 1974, p. 28.

[34] *Capital,* vol. 1, p. 79.

[35] *German Ideology,* p. 41.

[36[*Grundrisse,* p. 712.

[37] *German Ideology,* pp. 40, 80, 164, 671.

[38] Preface to *A Contribution to the Critique of Political Economy,* London, Lawrence & Wishart, 1971 [hereafter cited as 1859 Preface].

[39] For contrasting views see G. A. Cohen *Karl Marx's Theory of History: A Defence,* Oxford, Clarendon Press, 1978; E. P. Thompson *The Poverty of Theory,* London, Merlin, 1978; M. Godelier 'Infrastructures, Societies and History', *Current Anthropology* **19**(4), 1978; D. Sayer 'Method and Dogma in Historical Materialism', *Sociological Review,* **23**(4), 1975, 'Precapitalist Societies and Modern Marxist Theory', *Sociology,* **11**(1), 1977, *Marx's Method* (2nd edition), Brighton, Harvester, and Atlantic Highlands, Humanities, 1983, pp. 77–78.

[40] See reference [39], plus P. Corrigan and D. Sayer 'How the Law Rules', in B. Fryer *et al.* (eds.), *Law, State and Society,* London, Croom Helm, 1981.

[41] *Poverty of Philosophy,* p. 154; cf. 'Moralising criticism and critical morality', *CW* 6, p. 337.

[42] *Grundrisse,* p. 489.

[43] *Wage Labour and Capital,* p. 28.

[44] For fuller discussion see Sayer references in reference [39].

[45] *Capital,* vol. 3, London, Lawrence & Wishart, 1971, p. 791.

[46] Ibid., p. 790.

[47] *Capital,* vol. 1, p. 77.

[48] *Grundrisse,* pp. 472, 492.

[49] See Godelier op.cit., Sayer op.cit. 1977; compare, on feudalism, R. Hilton 'Feudalism in Europe', *New Left Review,* **147.**

[50] *German Ideology,* p. 36.

[51] Compare formulations in 1859 Preface with *German Ideology,* p. 49, 417; *Capital,* vol. 1, p. 82n; *Civil War in France,* Peking FLP 1970, pp.

176–177; 'Eighteenth Brumaire of Louis Bonaparte', *CW* 11, pp. 127–128.

[52] A. MacIntyre, quoted in E. P. Thompson 'Open letter to L. Kolakowski', *Socialist Register 1973*, London, Merlin, p. 97, n. 20.

[53] *Civil War in France*, p. 191; Economic and philosophic mss, p. 311.

[54] See further D. Sayer 'The critique of politics and politcal economy: capitalism, communism and the state in Marx's writings of the mid-1840s', *Sociological Review*, 33(2), 1985.

[55] *German Ideology*, p. 31.

[56] *Capital*, vol. 3, p. 791.

[57] *German Ideology*, p. 40.

[58] Ibid., p. 44.

[59] *Capital*, vol. 1, p. 75. Consider, for instance, how patriarchal family relations are simply *assumed* in the way Marx calculates the value of (male) labour-power in the same text: 'the sum of the means of subsistence necessary for the production of labour-power must include the means necessary for the labourer's substitutes, i.e., his children, in order that this race of peculiar commodity owners may perpetuate its appearance in the market' (ibid., p. 172). Quite a history is 'glossed' here; Barrett and McIntosh 'The Family Wage', *Capital and Class*, 11, 1980, discuss this problem further — and bring out the degree to which the male breadwinner is *not* the norm in modern capitalism.

[60] For a historical perspective on this see P. Corrigan and D. Sayer *The Great Arch: English State Formation as Cultural Revolution*, London and New York, Basil Blackwell, 1985.

[61] *Grundrisse*, p. 712.

[62] *German Ideology*, p. 31n.

[63] Ibid., p. 42n.

[64] See, e.g., ibid., pp. 51, 58, 135.

[65] Ibid., p. 52. Compare Marx's criticism of Proudhon in his 1869 Preface to the 2nd edition of his Eighteenth Brumaire, in D. Fernbach (ed.), *Surveys from Exile*, London, Penguin, 1973, p. 144.

[66] In *German Ideology*, pp. 659–660.

[67] Ibid.

[68] Economic and philosophic mss, p. 98.

[69] 1859 Preface.

[70] *Surveys from Exile*, p. 148.

[71] 1859 Preface.

[72] *German Ideology*, p. 92.

[73] See further Sayer, *Marx's Method*, pp. 83ff.

[74] For a sophisticated defence of this interpretation see Cohen, *Karl Marx's Theory of History*.

[75] *German Ideology,* p. 41.

[76] Ibid., p. 40n.

[77] Ibid., p. 91.

[78] Ibid., p. 319.

[79] See, *inter alia, Capital,* vol. 1, chs. 13 and 14; *Theories of Surplus Value,* Part I, London, Lawrence & Wishart 1969, Addenda; *Grundrisse,* p. 706; and above all the ms 'Results of the Immediate Process of Production', with 1976 Penguin edition of *Capital,* vol. 1, especially pp. 1019–1038. Many of the relevant passages are quoted and discussed in Sayer, *Marx's Method,* pp. 83–87.

[80] *German Ideology,* p. 46.

[81] Ibid., pp. 33–34. Picking up the theme of the 'abstract individual' discussed above, Marx adds that people are 'only by this fact put into a position to enter into relation with one another *as individuals*'.

[82] Ibid., p. 90.

[83] *Grundrisse,* p. 706.

[84] The arguments very briefly summarized here are elaborated in Sayer, *Marx's Method* (including the 1983 Afterword).

[85] See his *Poverty of Theory.*

[86] *Capital,* vol. 2, London, Lawrence & Wishart 1967, p. 229.

[87] 1859 Preface.

[88] *Capital,* vol. 1, pp. 79–80.

[89] See, *inter alia, Capital,* vol. 1, pp. 77, 236ff., 539–540, 568ff.; vol. 3, pp. 790ff.; *Theories of Surplus Value,* part 3, Moscow 1971, p. 484; *Wages, Price and profit,* Peking, FLP, 1973, pp. 50–52.

[90] *Capital,* vol. 3, p. 313.

[91] *Capital,* vol. 1, p. 75.

[92] See reference [84].

[93] General Introduction to *Grundrisse,* pp. 100ff.

[94] *Wage, Labour and Capital,* p. 28.

[95] *Capital,* vol. 3, p. 246.

[96] Ibid., p. 814; cf. vol. 1, p. 776.

[97] *Capital,* vol. 1, p. 169.

[98] *Theories of Surplus Value,* part 3, p. 275.

[99] *Capital,* vol. 1, parts 3 and 4; see also part 8.

[100] *Grundrisse,* pp. 460–461.

[101] *Capital,* vol. 1, part 8.

[102] *German Ideology,* p. 31.

[103] E. P. Thompson, *The Making of the English Working Class,* London, Penguin, 1969, pp. 9–11. The masculinity of the language is perhaps unfortunate.

Conclusion: Open Questions

Let us stay, for a moment, with Karl Marx. There is a well known discussion, in his General Introduction of 1857, of the historicity of the apparently abstract fundamental categories of another distinctively modern science, political economy [1]. The concept of labour, for example, from one point of view 'expresses an immeasurably ancient relation valid in all forms of society'. People work everywhere, they always have. Nevertheless, Marx goes on, in another sense 'the abstraction of the category "labour", "labour as such", labour pure and simple [...] achieves practical truth as an abstraction only as a category of the most modern society'. Only with modern capitalism do different concrete forms of work become abstractly equatable simply as the mere expenditure of labour-power. 'This example of labour', Marx concludes,

> shows strikingly how even the most abstract categories, despite their validity — precisely because of their abstractness — for all epochs, are nevertheless, in the specific character of this abstraction, themselves likewise a product of historic relations, and possess their full validity only for and within these relations.

In this sense, Marx continues, 'human anatomy contains a key to the anatomy of the ape'. Only with the bourgeois economy can analytic categories of sufficient abstraction be developed which allow access to, and comparative study of, economies in general.

Similar observations can be made regarding the concept of society. In one respect — as the most general of all sociological abstractions — society is merely that which links individuals to one another everywhere, whatever that may be. As such, the concept may become very abstract indeed: the mere unintended consequence or residuum of individual actions, or the formal structures of sociation, as cursory readings of Weber and Simmel respectively might suggest. At this level of abstraction it is questionable whether the concept refers to any real object at all. But at the same time, as we showed in Chapter 1, the very possibility of abstractly conceptualizing society at all would seem to have been historically dependent upon the concrete development of *bürgerliche Gesellschaft*: market society, civil society, bourgeois society. Only then did the generality *society* become visible, a possible object of theory, in a way comparable to the emergence of the *polis* as an object of reflection for the Greeks.

It is worth briefly reminding ourselves of these concrete sociological presuppositions of the ostensibly abstract concept of society, before returning to the abstraction itself. For none of the theories of society we have considered — including those where society is an absent concept — have succeeded in wholly eradicating their origins in *bürgerliche Gesellschaft*, however abstract and universal their pretentions may have been. Even in — perhaps especially in — the most apparently formalistic of sociologies, in which society characteristically reduces to sociation, the birthmarks of civil society are still there. If Winch (or Marx) is right and ideas are internally bound up with forms of life, it could hardly be otherwise. Consider Weber's ideal-types of action, where *Zweckrationalität* — the most perfectly formally rational type of action — has its ideal presupposition in the capitalist market, as Weber himself acknowledges [2]. But there is also a more particular point to be made here.

In many traditions — whether from the political left or the right — society is negatively evaluated, and contrasted unfavourably with something else, usually community: whether the real or imagined community of the past or the ideal community of the future. Misreadings of Tönnies are highly instructive in this context. Evidently it is bourgeois society which is at issue here. There are few unambiguously affirmative sociologies of *bürgerliche Gesellschaft*, even in the eighteenth century — indeed ironically it is Marx who in certain moods writes most rhapsodically about its historic achievements. Theorizing society is inseparable, in most nineteenth century sociology, from moral or political reflection on the conditions of human happiness. The invariable context of that reflection is the novelty, the very *modernity*, of society; the acute awareness, flashing up at a moment of danger (to use Benjamin's phrase), of the old world turned upside down, and something new — and unknown, and frequently terrifying — being born. Response varied from overtly reactionary, to revolutionary, to liberal and accommodative. Nevertheless Scheler's characterization of society as the detritus left by the disintegration of community, Marx's project for the overcoming of alienation — the 'naked cash-nexus between man and man' — by the restoration of communism on a higher basis, Weber's agonizing over the ethics of individual responsibility in the face of the iron cage of a disenchanted world, Durkheim's earnest concern to moralize modernity: all (like Comte, or Saint-Simon, or Simmel) recognizably share an urgency that comes from seeing society — though they might not use the phrase — as a *problem*.

In the twentieth century — more accurately perhaps, since 1918 — things seem to have changed. Though sociology may acknowledge, and study, social problems, society as such is no longer seen as a problem; indeed society as such is rarely glimpsed at all. It is tempting, but beyond our remit, to speculate upon the possible reasons for this. The habituation of modernity perhaps, the obliteration of memory and contrast, the achievement by *bürgerliche Gesellschaft* of the taken-for-granted obviousness of 'natural, self-understood forms of social life' [3], so that it no longer seems so remarkable, so novel, so threatening (or if threatening, is inexorably so, as for Weber)? Or simply the professionalization of sociology on the basis of a conception of science which relegates inquiries into society to the category of metaphysics? What is undeniable is the result.

To the question 'What is sociology?, the usual sociologists' answer — still — remains 'the study of society'. Yet the paradox is that for most of the twentieth century — the century in which, arguably, sociology first disentangled itself from social philosophy and became something approximating the empirical discipline which Comte, Durkheim, Marx, Weber, Simmel, and the other 'founding fathers' had all in their different ways wished it to be — sociology has in fact not been this at all. 'Society' has proved too grand an abstraction by far for modern sociological tastes. Instead we have reached a point where — outside the abstract heights of the philosophy of social science, as in for instance the recent work of Roy Bhaskar — to reflect on the concept of society at all, let alone to develop full-blooded theories of society, has become almost anachronistic. As we remarked at the outset of this book, a search for serious reflections on society — as distinct from reflections on *Vergesellschaftung* — will take us back beyond the *fin de siècle*. There are occasional, and notable modern exceptions to this, like the work of Winch or the Frankfurt school. There have also been attempts critically to synthesize the classics, as with Parsons, Berger and Luckmann, or latterly Giddens; but these only obliquely prove the point in the very classicism of their starting-point. It is fair to say that the study of society has not, in the main, been a twentieth-century sociological preoccupation. Sociology has busied itself with other, less grandiose matters.

To the question, then, 'Does sociology need to ground itself in a concept of society?' an empirical answer would have to be resoundingly in the negative. Sociology can apparently get by perfectly well without society. Indeed a more than plausible case can be made for saying that sociological knowledge has progressed to the extent that the discipline has at last liberated itself from fruitless speculation on society as such — however conceived — and turned its attention to the empirical study of real instances of human sociation.

And yet: is this all there is to be said on the issue? We suggest not.

This book did not set out to answer the question 'What is society?', but simply to review (some) other people's answers. Nevertheless, it does provide grounds for suggesting that the question itself should not be so readily dismissed as it has come to be. There are various reasons for this. As we showed at the end of Chapter 3, a refusal to conceptualize society within sociology, as in many 'action theories', may merely evade the problems to which a concept of society is the attempted answer. Indeed these problems — and with them singularly reified notions of society — tend often tacitly to resurface in the guise of a philosophy of history providing speculative answers to the questions which the initial exclusion of reflection on society rules out of court. Or as the perspectives addressed in Chapter 4 powerfully suggest, the very conditions under which meaningful individual action and interaction can intelligibly be conceived at all are arguably only those of the real existence of society. In addition to such internal criticisms of perspectives within which society is an absent concept, we must take into account the positive arguments advanced for the sui generis reality of society, however conceived, by theorists for whom the indispensability of the concept is not in dispute, most notably Durkheim (whether or not one accepts his own view of society).

A survey such as this therefore remains worthwhile. And if it cannot answer the question 'What is society?', it may suggest, perhaps, not only — itself an important conclusion — that sociology may yet have much to gain from returning to the question itself, but also what kind of constraints need to be respected by any putative answer. If a refusal to theorize society seems to us ultimately an evasion of what is arguably the central analytic issue of sociology — its object of inquiry, that feature of the world which grounds it as a discipline — then none of the positive theories of society examined here seems to us to be wholly satisfactory either. All, however, have their merits.

In brief, we would suggest than an adequate concept of society must minimally acknowledge: society's transcendent facticity, its objective status, *vis-à-vis* individuals, without at the same time unacceptably reifying it; society's ideality, its character as intercommunicable understandings, rules, meanings, without wholly idealizing it; and society's material anchorage in human interchange with nature, and linked (if not reducible) to this, society's historicity, without thereby collapsing it into an economic reductionism. Due weight might also be given to society's moral character, without in the process denying its internal differentiatedness. None of the theories of society we have considered acknowledge all these things, all recognize some of them. Some synthesis is clearly required. But the synthesis might make for some strange bedfellows.

One of the more interesting points to emerge from our study is the way in which, on close examination, standard stereotypes blur, dissolve, and break down. It is conventional to dichotomize, to speak for instance of 'the two sociologies' — of action and of structure — in the title of Alan Dawe's famous article. Recent Marxist work (for instance Bhaskar) often accepts the same dichotomy, and then goes on to argue that historical materialism resolves the structure/action antinomy. But — as we hope this study has shown, if it has done nothing else — in reality things are far more complicated than this. Durkheim, for example, in one aspect the positivist who (rightly) occasions Winch's ire, in another aspect must be seen as pioneering a concept of society as idea which is in many ways remarkably similar to Winch's own. Winch situates himself squarely within the Weberian tradition of action analysis, yet ends up rejecting the methodological individualism fundamental to that tradition. Many of his statements about the relation between forms of life and the ideas they embody are remarkably close to the pronoucements of that materialist *par excellence* Karl Marx, who also anticipated Durkheim's views on the social origin and paradigms of the logical categories. Durkheim's enduring concern with society as moral order finds unexpected echoes in Abel's and Habermas's analysis of the normative presuppositions of communication. Marx, Winch and Simmel all concur in a conception of society as a set of relations. And so on.

These and other issues come to mind when we raise once more the issue of the nature of society and its connections with sociology. We will have succeeded in our modest aim, if the reader too is persuaded to return to the problem of 'society's vexatiousness' (Dahrendorf), to the 'puzzling life of society' (Simmel), to 'the product of human reciprocal action' (Marx).

REFERENCES

[1] Marx, *Grundrisse*, London, Penguin, 1973, pp. 100–108.
[2] Weber, *Economy and Society*, (ed. by G. Roth and C. Wittich), Berkeley, University of California Press, 1978, vol. 1, p. 635.
[3] Marx, *Capital*, vol. 1, London, Lawrence & Wishart, 1970, p. 75.

Further Reading

These suggestions for further reading are intended largely to indicate some of the major texts we have discussed and some of the introductory and key works which the reader might find useful. More detailed references are contained in the notes to each chapter.

For general works that deal analytically with some of the issues raised here see:

R. Bhaskar, *The Possibility of Naturalism*, Brighton, Harvester Press, 1979 (esp. ch. 2).

R. Keat and
   J. Urry, *Social Theory as Science*, 2nd edn, London and Boston, Routledge, 1982.

T. Benton, *Philosophical Foundations of the Three Sociologies*, London and Boston, Routledge, 1977.

W. Outhwaite, *Concept Formation in Social Science*, London and Boston, Routledge, 1983.

As an introduction to concepts of society see:

T. Campbell, *Seven Theories of Human Society*, Oxford, Oxford University Press, 1981.

L. A. Coser, *Masters of Sociological Thought*, 2nd edn, New York, Chicago, San Francisco and Atlanta, Harcourt Brace Jovanovich, 1977.

For Durkheim see:

E. Durkheim, *The Rules of Sociological Method* (ed. and introd. by Steven Lukes; trans. by W. D. Halls), London and Basingstoke, Macmillan, 1982.

R. N. Bellah (ed.), *Emile Durkheim on Morality and Society*, Chicago, University of Chicago Press, 1973.

A. Giddens, *Emile Durkheim: Selected Writings*, Cambridge, Cambridge University Press, 1972.

S. Lukes, *Emile Durkheim. His Life and Work*, London, Allen Lane, 1973.

K. Thompson, *Emile Durkheim*, Chichester, Ellis Horwood and Tavistock, 1982.

K. Thompson, *Readings from Emile Durkheim*, Chichester, Ellis Horwood and Tavistock, 1985.

For society as absent concept see:

K. H. Wolff (ed.), *Essays on Sociology, Philosophy and Aesthetics by Georg Simmel, et al.*, Columbus, Ohio, Ohio State University Press, 1958 (see especially the essays: 'The Problem of Sociology' and 'How is Society Possible?').

D. N. Levine (ed.), *Georg Simmel, On Individuality and Social Forms*, Chicago, University of Chicago Press, 1971.

D. Frisby, *Georg Simmel*, Chichester, Ellis Horwood and Tavistock, 1984.

M. Weber, *Economy and Society* (ed. by G. Roth and C. Wittich), Berkeley, Los Angeles and London, University of California Press, 1978 (esp. vol. 1, part 1).

T. Burger, *Max Weber's Theory of Concept Formation*, Durham, North Carolina, Duke University Press, 1976.

A. Schutz, *The Phenomenology of the Social World* (trans. G. Walsh and F. Lehnert), Evanston, Northwestern University Press, 1967.

For society as idea and ideal see:

E. Durkheim, *The Elementary Forms of the Religious Life*, London, Allen & Unwin, 1915.

P. Winch, *The Idea of a Social Science*, London, Routledge; New York, Humanities Press, 1958.

K.-0. Apel, *Towards a Transformation of Philosophy* (trans. G. Adey and D. Frisby), London/Boston, Routledge, 1980.

T. McCarthy, *The Critical Theory of Jürgen Habermas*, Cambridge, Mass., MIT Press; Cambridge, Polity, 1984.

For society as second nature see:

K. Marx and
  F. Engels, *The German Ideology*, London, Lawrence & Wishart, 1965.
K. Marx, *Early Writings* (introd. by L. Coletti, trans. by R. Livingstone and G. Benton), Harmondsworth, Penguin, 1975.
T. Bottomore and
  M. Rubel, *Karl Marx: Selected Writings in Sociology and Social Philosophy* (2nd edn), Harmondsworth, Penguin, 1963.
D. Sayer, *Marx's Method* (2nd edn), Brighton, Harvester Press; New Jersey, Humanities Press, 1983.

For attempted syntheses of the classical traditions of theorizing society see:

T. Parsons, *The Structure of Social Action*, New York, NcGraw-Hill, 1937.
P. Berger and
  T. Luckmann, *The Social Construction of Reality*, New York, Doubleday, 1966.
A. Giddens, *The Constitution of Society*, Cambridge, Polity, 1984.

Index

Guildford College
Learning Resource Centre

Please return on or before the last date shown
This item may be renewed by telephone unless overdue

1 4 APR 2005		
2 3 FEB 2006		
2 9 MAR 2008		

Class: _301.24 FRI_

Title: _Society_

Author: _FRISBY, David_

Harris Centre LRC

137722